Struggle in a Secular Age

Struggle in a Secular Age

Clashes of Christian Body and Soul

Dr. Larry D. Harwood

CWI

Christian World Imprints™

First Published, 2013

ISBN: 978-81-925121-0-5

Christian World Imprints™
Christian Publishing & Books from India
H-12 Bali Nagar, New Delhi-110015
info@kkagencies.com
www.ChristianWorldImprints.com
More at: www.kkagencies.co.in/sitemap
Phone: +91 11 25465925 Fax: +91 11 25173055

Printed at Chawla Offset Printers

For Elspeth Lillian

The Author

Dr. Larry D. Harwood is Professor of Philosophy and Religious Studies at Viterbo University in La Crosse, Wisconsin, USA, and specializes in Philosophy of Religion, Asian Philosophy, History of Religion, and Religion and Aesthetics. In addition to fictional writing, he has published articles on Nietzsche, Bertrand Russell, C.S. Lewis, Confucianism, postmodernism, the problem of evil, and the meaning of life. His book entitled *Denuded Devotion to Christ: The Ascetic Piety of Protestant True Religion in the Reformation* is scheduled for publication by Wipf and Stock in 2013, and he is currently at work on a book on Bertrand Russell and religion. In the spring term of 2008 he was an American Fulbright Scholar at the University of Lisbon, Portugal, where he taught in the Program in Theory of Literature. In 2004 he made the first of several trips to Asia and has returned on three occasions bringing in tow almost forty students.

The Book

This book is a collection of short stories depicting spiritual struggle within the contours of sobering and sometimes fatal situations. Some stories portray less serious and humorous situations, though with redemptive themes still intertwined. The characters and situations presented do not disappoint the reader's desire for pleasurable reading, though a sense of the fleeting world mixed with spiritual confrontation or confusion may give the reader pause before moving to the next story. For readers who like realistic religious fiction with plausible characters in trying circumstances, the book provides a variety of stories in the contest of wills between living for wrong things and the confrontations inevitable with a calling in Christ. While some stories within this book have this explicit context, others provide samples of the infinite battles that confront the believer living in a secular or distorted age.

Acknowledgements

The author kindly acknowledges permission to reprint the following stories:

"Honor Thy Brother," first published in *Windhover* 7, 2002; "The Squatter," first published in *The Dead Mule*, September, 2005; "The Saints," first published in *VerbSap*, April, 2006; "Railing at the Parson," first published in *Branchwood Journal*, Spring/Summer 2006; "The Daughter-in-Law," first published in *Southern Gothic Online*, November, 2006; "Arrogance," first published in *The Houston Literary Review*, June 2008; "Wise as Serpents," first published in *Canopic Jar 21*, July 2008; "Lost Daughter," first published in *Touchstone* Volume 75, 2011.

Preface

In this work I make no literary pretensions. A philosopher by training, I only came to serious interest in fictional stories while a graduate student in philosophy. Eventually I tried my hand at writing fiction, but only because I was more assured of the power of the form than my own ability to use it.

In my circles and experience, philosophers as a group do not write or read much fiction, though I am told the situation is somewhat different with philosophers and scholars in Eastern Europe. I am not sure about India. Nevertheless, I eventually developed a belated love for fiction, whereas previously fiction had needlessly meandered for me as a philosopher. Philosophy had been preferred because philosophy had cut to the chase, peeled the onion, as I often say to my students now. Continuing with the onion analogy, philosophy can provoke one to desperation or tears. Small wonder one has few fireside chats around it—mostly it is you and the fire. As Iris Murdoch, the late British philosopher and novelist surmised, philosophy is unnatural, upsetting, deflationary often—only a few can tolerate, indeed enjoy this kind of scrutiny, or mind that the questions of philosophy remain despite our best efforts, questions. I tell students that it is not so much a good mind that is needed for philosophy, though that is the case, but also a good stomach. Philosophy can be wrenching.

Fictional works, so long neglected in my life, suddenly seemed to be about the real world. This was the attraction I felt for fiction and thus the motivation that provoked me to eventually tilt toward trying the form. I came to realize that our disciplines can narrow our world, that is, us—so too, my own world of the discipline of philosophy, though usually thought of as stupendously magnificent, however befuddling for the uninitiated. So too, probably in a different and older culture, I might not have had the kind of jolting awakening I did on discovering fiction. However, in my American experience, many philosophers insisted on scrutinizing the questions of philosophy directly by emptying them of the context in which one encounters them. Suddenly I was finding the context hugely interesting.

On my first attempts to write fiction, during the summers and away from formal philosophy for a while, I would meander across my parent's farm fields while thinking about how to develop the story I was laboring at writing. When I came up with something I thought significant it was an ecstatic experience. Meanwhile, my dad would have gone away to market to sell some farm products, and tell me to "stay busy" while he was gone. I did—but walking the fields and thinking about fiction, rather than weeding or repairing fences or the hundreds of other jobs necessary to maintain a farm. And then I read about William Faulkner's writing some of his work while he was a postmaster in Oxford, Mississippi. And I did not feel so alone or different—but oh, such pretensions, Faulkner, Harwood—I didn't even have his initials. Nevertheless, I was inside a world now that was new to me and enthralling, and it has not since worn off.

Larry D. Harwood
La Crosse, Wisconsin, USA
September, 2012

Contents

1

Honor Thy Brother

The soldier reached across puddles of water to magazines loaded with bullets and dripping with water. The canteen lay between sandbags on top, making more room in the crowded foxhole below, but savage rifles had ripped holes in the water container and the falling piece spewed water over the hole. He did not bother with the carcass, though it interfered with his boot traffic and was emptying all his drinking water into an already soggy hole. He kicked at the canteen to get it out of his way and slammed a water-beaded magazine into his weapon, guessing if the weapon would still fire. The rifle bolt sucked another waiting round into the firing chamber as he nudged up one side of the foxhole, but worn boot bottoms slipped in the mud as his body fell forward, and he made preparations to collide with a wall of earth. There was no one to tell him he could surrender, and no communication left anyway—except for shouting to the next foxhole. He pulled the rifle close to his body and stiffened his neck, hoping to cushion his fall with the helmet on his lowered head. A round went off in the impact and he paused to check his weapon and made mental count of how much ammunition remained, though he knew that nothing in the tiny hole could help. He shouted to the next foxhole, but things were no better there.

He crouched beside the earthen wall and extended the weapon over his head, in an effort to offer resistance to his attackers. The trim rifle barrel dropped into a crevice between two sandbags and without benefit of sight or specific target he squeezed the trigger and waited for his erratic rifle to expend the last round. There was no noise, for the deafening blasts from enemy guns made hearing impossible. His weapon was still after fifteen seconds of rapid fire and he jerked it back down beside him, tossed the empty magazine into one corner of the foxhole and shoved in another full one. He planted the rifle in the same position, but the first round misfired and he jerked the weapon back down in the hole and fumbled with the stock of his weapon while he prayed. He exhaled a huge breath and leaned back on the opposite wall and rested against the soft cool earth. He stared at his weapon, but finally pulled the magazine out of the tired rifle.

The barrel smoked from end to end from too much firing too fast, and he would wait for the rifle to cool while he counted ammunition again. He mistook a box of food for ammunition until he found ham and eggs, and jelly and crackers and a plastic knife and fork inside. A small smile spread across his greasy face and he said another prayer.

He watched oily smoke waft up from the hot barrel as he sat down in the soggy bottom of his foxhole to serve up his meal. A disturbance from above sent his eyes upward, but billows of gray and black smoke hid a sky scarcely visible anymore. He listened to a radio still working while he worked, but communication had fallen into hostile hands and enemy soldiers now used it to taunt any remaining soldiers. He listened to the chatter for a few seconds and reached to turn the radio off. Dirt kicked up at the top of his foxhole from enemy fire, and the white handkerchief placed for his meal was already littered by falling debris from above and soaked by dingy water below. He removed his helmet and bowed his head while dirt and debris fell into his hair. He pushed long muscular legs forward in the square hole and settled boot heels into soft soil walls. The cool earth stole some of the heat from his sweaty jacket and he shut his eyes for the small comfort of heat draining from his upper body.

There was nothing left to drink, so he used the canteen carcass to scoop up water from the bottom of the hole. He ate the crackers and jelly first and though the order was odd, it was his habit, and why break habit now he thought. The eggs were next and they were scrambled, the way he always preferred them. He had not asked for any other kind of eggs in two years. The ham was watery, and so he did not have to ruin good meat by drinking too much dirty water. After his last swallow he bowed his head again and made the sign of the cross.

He wished to see his sister once more. She was his only sibling, and she had written him every day, even though she was married now. He had shared so much of his life with her after their parents had been killed and he knew she would die for a while when she heard about him. He wanted to tell her how much she was a part of him. Of course he had told her and very many times in letters of the past year. He knew too that she would want him to spend his last bit of life on something other than her and he pulled out a grease pencil from his belongings and grabbed one of the small cardboard ammo boxes and dumped the shiny cartridges in the sticky mud of his foxhole. He pulled the box apart and made it flat and started to pencil words across the thin cardboard. Flying dirt and debris continued to rain down into his foxhole and he brushed the box clean with a sleeve as he scribbled. The roar of mechanized tracked vehicles came closer while the quiet noise of small arms fire receded. If he had not fired out of his foxhole they might not even know he was there, and by now his foxhole was almost covered with falling debris. Maybe they would miss him or perhaps forget him. When he finished writing, he shouted to the next hole, but he heard no voices except the one within.

"We had fire from there," a voice barked, as the long arm of a husky soldier pointed to bumpy ground. His soldiers, expert in attention to the unusual, missed nothing that appeared either suspicious or probable and each of them readied themselves, with fingers close to triggers and eyes trained to spot the slightest twitch of any movement. Two of them took a hand signal from him to walk forward while the others stood fast and waited. As necessary precaution grenades were lobbed down holes on their mop-up operation and the foxholes in front of them received one each. The force of simultaneous explosions shook the earth under their feet, but also provided comfort that nothing hostile remained in the dens in front of them. The impact brought one body up for an instant before it slid back effortlessly, while the other stopped, its downward flight checked by a tree root that held the suspended body by a strap of clothing. The soldiers smiled and passed by the holes.

The last of six soldiers stopped while the others walked backwards in his direction and separated their trigger fingers from their eyes for an interlude of amusement. A piece of cardboard with writing jutted from the jacket of the soldier whose lifeless body lay sideways in the hole in the earth. The piece was fixed around a jacket button and poked with holes, but the inquisitive soldiers were too curious about the scribbling to mind a few decapitated letters or the extra work required to see what a dead man had done as his last deed. Each of them poked their head over the top of the foxhole, trying to make out the writing. When they began to raise their voices the squad leader signaled for silence.

He reached down into the foxhole and grasped the piece of cardboard punched with holes. There was warm blood on it and he reached further to feel the flesh of a body whose soul was just leaving. He unfastened the pocket button to free the cardboard and rubbed the mutilated piece across the ground, turning it one direction, then another, and then turning it sideways. He stared at the scribbling without words and without making any words out, but when he did, he read them with stiff silent lips while his head dropped.

He reached to place the cardboard piece back in the hole.

"Take a look," the leader ordered, while he remained on his knees. The five soldiers leaned over the hole in the ground. Their dour faces contorted as they twisted their heads and finally looked in desperation at their squad leader. They were too embarrassed to ask him to read words they could not, but he read them anyway. He made the sign of the cross and ordered them to move out.

2

The Squatter

John's mother handed her son his wife's note. He eased back on the five gallon bucket rubbing his fishing pole with orange resin and whistled.

"Don't look good for you," she said.

He plopped his fishing line into still water.

"Why you say that?" he said.

"Read it," she answered.

The tip of his fishing pole zipped down, and he struggled before jerking the line up. A bass dripping with water droplets and green algae dangled from the flying end of his cane pole.

"Would you look at that!" he said.

"You going to read it or not?"

"I'm gonna eat it. When we had something like that on our plates? Good thing I came down here. We'll be eatin' high, tonight."

"You might."

"What you mean?" He stared at the woman.

"Anything scare you?" she asked.

He dropped his jaw as he unhooked the fish.

"Nothing. You're the one who raised me. You know that."

"So I did."

He laughed as he swept algae from the fish with his hand.

"You gonna look at that letter?"

"I know what's in it."

"Why you reckoned she left again?"

"Don't matter," he said, gawking at his catch, and trying to measure it with his hand.

His mother shoved him into the water. "Lazy you is; stupid you ain't." He fell backwards, as his fingers gripped the fish's mouth.

"What's that about?" he said, sitting in water with cattails brushing against his face.

"Don't act stupid. Lazy you is; stupid you ain't."

"I heard the first time," he shouted.

"You living on borrowed time."

"She'll be back," he said.

"She always comes back, does she?"

"Where'd you say you caught it?" she asked.

"I told you, behind them tails," he answered.

"What you using?"

"Plastic, black worm."

"Anymore down there?"

"Don't know. We can go again in the morning."

"I'll be gone then."

"Gone?"

"You don't know what gone means?"

"I don't know what you mean."

"I bought me a ticket this afternoon. I reckon you were occupied with fishing, or readin' my letter."

"Ticket?"

"Yea. You read it, didn't you?"

He starred at her, and pushed back uncombed hair.

"You said you bought a ticket."

"You read the letter, did ya?"

He flinched. "The letter got lost when I fell, in the water. Maybe a fish ate it or something."

"She didn't tell you? I mean she didn't tell you?" She snickered.

"Tell me what?"

"Better than I figured."

"What?"

"I said better than I figured."

"I heard. What you done did Sarah?"

"I told you, I bought a ticket, outta here."

"Did what? Quit beating around the bush woman!"

"She sold the place."

He stopped eating and looked out the window.

"Sold what?"

"This place."

"She can't do that, just up and sell. This place means something, something to me anyway." He looked out the window again, as his fish started to get cold.

"No, ain't seen him for a couple days now, sheriff. She told me I might have trouble from him. Don't know that they did right by him though. I mean them up and leaving him like that."

"If he comes on the property again you can call me."

"If I have a mind to, I will," he said. Ab Runn, the new owner, didn't have a mind to, but when John Surd showed up again, Runn did assess him from the window of the house. He had little else to do, so he sat by the window and watched the lanky figure maneuver around the pond. Runn had little idea why the boy's mother sold the place now, lock stock and barrel. She took only her clothes, and left everything else, and told him if he bought the place he'd have enough stuff to set up housekeeping. Runn couldn't figure the woman selling in such haste. He'd wanted the place for years, in fact asked her if she would sell it many times, with no thought he'd ever have it. Too bad it was so close to the end of him when she called. Said she had to "move on" and was taking her daughter-in-law with her.

Runn didn't ask questions—wasn't the type—not his affair, but he wondered when she told him about her son. She had smiled a little, made him curious, though he had not seen Surd till two days ago walking around the pond. Runn didn't particularly mind that, though the sheriff told him he should watch him. Said the boy had been in some trouble before, stealing.

Runn patted his dog as he watched the boy groping around the shallow end of the pond, and finally resting himself on a five gallon bucket. Surd wiped his face; that was understandable, it was hot out there. The visitor sat for a half hour, throwing pieces of weed in the water, and looking like he was lost. The warm sun must have got to him, because he fell off his bucket after a while. Runn was in no shape to get outside the house without help. The old man scarcely walked anymore, so when the boy just lay in the water, Runn decided to let his dog out of the house to see if his visitor was okay.

Surd moved when the dog approached and he pulled himself back up onto his bucket. After that he got his fishing pole up. Runn's dog scampered back to the house.

When Surd came back the next day, Runn decided he'd better send the fellow a note. Runn kept a bulky collar on his dog and managed to wrap his note around the dog's collar, with a big "For You" scribbled on the outside. He watched from the window as the dog scampered down to the pond where Surd sat on his bucket. Runn watched the man pull the note out.

Surd must have written his letters with a little mud and a twig and then let the piece of paper dry in the sun. Runn's eyes were about as gone as his legs, but he did make out the nine reddish words etched on the paper after an hour. The old man dropped the paper, and hated he had bought the place:

"My momma and wife run off. I got nothing."

Surd came back with some cardboard and his five gallon bucket the next day, but Runn didn't figure the entire plan until Surd put it together. The boy built a shelter for himself with the cardboard. It was hot out there, fiercely hot, but Runn still didn't get that the boy intended the covering to house him during the day and night too. It was obvious that the wanderer had been sleeping and staying who knows where before, so the next morning Runn sent another note around the dog collar, telling Surd it was okay for him to stay there, but Surd sent him a longer message back. The writing this time was in ink:

"The raw earth is hard on the flesh. If you aren't using that old car up there could you bring it down here?"

Surd had a good handwriting, and Runn wondered how much school he had with penmanship as neat and pretty as any he had ever seen. The old man had a car, but he never drove it anymore because his legs couldn't exert the strength to work the pedals, so he tied the keys around the dog's collar and sent the animal down to Surd's place at the water. Runn had had someone drive the jalopy over when he moved into the new place. But Surd didn't drive either, and wrote him back a note to that effect. The note was actually a letter, for Surd went on to explain that there was a big tree nearby where he had built his cardboard shack, and that if he gave the car just a little shove probably it would roll down the hill toward the pond and the tree would stop it before it went too far. Runn thought this a good idea, and wondered again how much schooling Surd had had, and what other kind of things the man had done with his education.

The car didn't stop where it was supposed to and wound up submerged, though not all of it. Water came up in the floorboard, but didn't reach the seats, so Surd did have some dry spots in his new place.

The gas in the tank started to leak out into the water a week later, and Surd noticed that he no longer had to fish anymore, because some of the fish started to come to the surface. They didn't taste good, though, Surd wrote to Runn, and when Runn sent him another note, Surd wrote back that he feared his only staple perishing soon and there'd be no fish for him to eat then. The old man couldn't have that and because there wasn't any cemetery on the place, Ab wrote Surd back and told him to come up and share his house.

That day Surd moved in, and the next day he went fishing.

3

The Saints

"Smells terrible!" she said.

"No worse than some people," he replied.

Any other time she would have laughed, but the stench smelled almost toxic as it spread closer to the couple already dirtied by their task.

"The coffin wasn't sealed!" she said.

His nose followed the scent and spotted the skunk before she spoke again.

"Course it was," he said, slightly annoyed, and he grabbed her hand and yanked her behind another stone with him to wait the guilty animal out.

"He'll go soon, and we'll get back to work," he said.

"I'm not so sure about this anymore Jim."

"You need to know. Stay with me, and we'll both see. You'll get to see him for yourself."

"I don't know anymore!" she said.

"We will in a minute. Soon as that animal goes far enough."

In little hurry, the skunk ambled over the pile of fresh soil and cast his nose into the digging hole as he sniffed at the earth. Jim remained anxious to finish, and tossed a rock in the direction of the furry creature that now scampered out of sight.

"Let's go," he said.

"I don't know Jim; will you listen to me!" she said.

"Look. Let's get this done. We can settle this thing—once and for all. We've got more work than digging earth." He smiled at her.

"I don't think we should be doing this," she said.

"You wanted to know; we can know!"

"Catholics don't have to dig to see it!"

"Well, we do—I mean you do. So we gotta get him up."

Carolyn Jones wanted to marry a Protestant boy, though she was fonder of him a week ago, and before she slipped and said Protestants had no saintly bodies, unlike some Catholic corpses that never decomposed after a life of holiness. Jim demurred.

She and her family had witnessed one in Rome two years earlier, and she had never forgotten. When he took issue with her—said Protestants had saints too— she brandished her Rome example, complete with two photographs and a postcard, but Jim Strusser shrugged, unmoved. He told her that Protestant bodies were as saintly as Catholic bodies, and he could prove it for her.

Her parents never cared for the boy.

"And why not?" she had inquired.

"Didn't like him from the first minute I laid eyes on him," her father said.

"Why?" she had demanded. When her father paused, went back to his paper, she left— stomped out—but he stopped her. She stood waiting, presuming he would say something more, maybe answer her question, something. He said nothing.

"No crucifix totted on his chest?" she offered, and her father, and then her mother too, erupted, and the screaming match stalemated after they prohibited the girl from seeing the boy again. She persisted despite their order.

The anxious couple prematurely settled on a Protestant lady. Gloria Hayes was revered in their community until two years ago, when her dead body slid down the right side of the pulpit, finished after a heart attack killed her before she concluded with the church announcements. Carolyn objected to the woman from the beginning, saying this candidate was exceptionally pious for a Protestant, and that Jim had claimed that all true Protestants were saints, and therefore, any Protestant should suffice as well as any other Protestant, and therefore they should examine one not so saintly. Gloria had a good logical mind, and Jim Strusser was in love and wanted Carolyn's hand in marriage, so he would do what it took to get her--and he consented to find a deceased that had not lived the godliest life, but had nevertheless, in Jim's words, "been washed by the Blood."

Jim felt doubts that Bob Savoy was the best choice for this venture now that he was about to see Savoy again. The man had gone to prison multiple times over his criminal career, but finally turned in all his sins at the cross, and became a new and changed man for two months exactly before a trailered vehicle hit and ran over him in the street. Jim knew good works didn't save a man, no matter how good, but Savoy was so bad before, he might take more redeeming than your average sinner.

"No, that ain't right," he said to himself, and he slapped his face.

"What you doing?" she asked.

"Bob Savoy was a saint, because of Jesus, and not because of himself," he said, now sufficiently chastened for his error with a reddened face.

"What you saying?" she asked.

"I'm saying we're opening him up—for you to see—and me."

Carolyn saw his resolve, knew no hope remained for trying to halt this boy sick with love for her, but she asked if they could pray first, and whether Jim could open the lid by himself, and she only look.

"That'll work for me," he said, and he slid his slight frame back beside the uncovered casket, after his prayer.

"Grave digging it was?"

"Yes Sir," Jim said.

"Mind telling me what you meant in disturbing the dead like that?"

"No harm intended, Sir. Only needed confirmation," he said.

"Confirmation? Of what?"

"Rather not say, Sir. Boy you're about to be charged with intent to commit murder. You better say something."

"I didn't harm her," he said.

"Don't look that way to us. Appears you was about to dispose of her in that casket. After you had surmised her state, that is," the officer said.

"No Sir," wasn't like that at all, Jim said.

"Well, how was it then?"

"I couldn't have got her in that thing, even if I wanted. Besides, I didn't hurt her—I love that girl," he said.

"Don't appear that way to her family nor to us."

"What?"

"You'll be charged with intent to kill that girl."

"She knows better!"

"Well she can't talk in that coma, now can she? And you, you won't talk."

"Okay. We I mean I wanted to see if Bob Savoy was a saint."

"A saint? He was a criminal; everybody knew that. A saint, son? We talking about the same man?" he asked.

"Yea," Jim said.

"Why you digging him up?"

"I had to see."

"See?" he asked.

"To see if he was a saint."

Jim Strusser claimed that when he pushed the coffin lid up the girl had passed out, and fell onto the edge of the hard steel. She had a large gash on her forehead, while the doctors worried about the state of her brain. Her face could be fixed.

Meanwhile the prosecutor made hay with Strusser's story about an accident, but Strusser stuck with his story, though his lawyer urged a plea bargain that Strusser rejected. It soon became clear that the boy chanced losing the case against him, and so Strusser's lawyer had recourse to a string of character witnesses on his client's behalf, but the chilling story of a grave digging, and a girl lying in a coma as a result proved too much to jurors who knew and respected the Jones's.

With hope receding for Strusser, his lawyer made another attempt to get the youngster a lighter sentence by pleading guilty to a lesser charge. The stubborn youth, however, refused again.

All might have been well, if the girl had recovered, had come out of the coma, but she didn't recover, not for a long time, and the boy went to prison for almost as long.

She hobbled when she walked, and Jim Strusser got out the wheelchair to navigate her around the stones more easily. The terrain of the cemetery was bumpy.

"Don't know exactly where they're at," she said. "I suppose somewhere with the rest of the Jones's," she continued.

The darkness didn't help, and a dim flashlight proved little aid, but eventually they found the graves.

"Sure you want to do this?" he asked.

"I'm sure," Carolyn said.

He was still as agile with a shovel as he had been before prison. He did not stop to rest until taking three feet of earth from the top of one of the graves.

"No need to open both," she said. "Either one will do," she added.

"Okay," he said, and he put his shovel back in the same hole, as he stared momentarily at the adjacent grave, and the marker that read Together Forever.

"Still sure you want to do this?" he asked again.

"Still sure," she said. Her graying hair was pulled back, and made her look older than her years.

"I'll be done soon, and we can get out of here," he said, as he threw another shovel of grave dirt on the mounting pile.

"No police will bother us tonight," she said.

"They're there," he said, nervously.

"They'll keep their distance," she said. A police car had pulled up to the cemetery, and the engine stopped as lights went off. Jim saw one inside the car with binoculars pointed their way.

"About done," he said. "Still sure?" he asked again.

"Yea," she said. "You?" she asked.

"No, don't think I can," he said.

"Dummes is there in the car. I expect he'll be willing to do it; I did say something to him about it, I mean that I might need his help." The woman's voice started to crack.

He tossed the shovel into the pile of dirt. The dirty coffin lid lay in plain view finally.

"Thank you," she said. "I'll let my parents rest after this—what rest is theirs; I just need to know," she added.

"I know," he said, and he leaned over her wheel chair and kissed her cheek.

"I won't be long," she said, after she returned the kiss.

He walked away.

She motioned toward the police car, and Jim walked toward Dummes, making his way toward Carolyn and the opened grave.

"Thanks," Jim said when the two met.

"Don't mention it," Dummes said. "You can sit in the car with my deputy if you want," he offered.

"No, I'll just wait for her here. But thanks," he said.

Dummes' age had hardly made him frail, and he easily broke the lid free of the box after a couple minutes of work. He looked back at Carolyn Strusser before he would open it further.

If the woman had not been present he might have set this corpse and the one beside it on fire himself.

She motioned.

Jim Strusser saw her head go into her lap when Dummes stepped out of her way.

Her wails pierced the night air, and the sparrows that habitually nested in the cedar trees roused themselves to move away from the noise. She called for Dummes to turn her chair around, and Jim came for her.

Dummes signaled his deputy to come to the grave, and the two of them began the work of filling the hole up again.

4

Railing at the Parson

None of the three hecklers showed after the fire, and none of their families filed a missing persons report.

The pastor was scarcely able to talk to anyone that week, while news sputtered and then spread to nearby towns, with the story filling area newspapers and television, and every reporter everywhere wanted comment from a man who refused interviews and visitors and remained holdup inside the parsonage. When members of his own congregation tried to visit, his wife answered the door to say that the man was in no condition to see anyone, and that he needed fervent prayer, though the request came from her and not from a man whom she said was scarcely in the world.

On the third day of his seclusion, his wife slipped a doctor into their home despite her husband's protest, and the pastor—after a protracted discussion with his wife—grudgingly admitted his visitor to a dark room with a grunt.

"And what can you do for me, bring my church back?"

"No, can't do that," the physician said, unable to miss quivering arms raised to heaven.

"Only God, by his power, and his power alone, can do anything for me!" the pastor said, and he began to scream.

His wife and the physician retreated back to the hallway after the noise became intolerable.

"I may be able to do something for you," the physician shouted back, prompted by the pastor's wife. He waited another minute, crouched low in the hallway.

"Can't say I can help. Does he have a psychiatrist?" He asked.

The pastor's wife showed him to the door after he declined payment.

Next day the pastor asked his wife to call the same physician again, and he apologized for his rudeness. The physician asked about his sleep.

"I'm not."

"I can prescribe something for that," he said.

"Do," the Pastor said, "I need what I can get. My wife too." He looked at his visitor. "She needs to understand. I mean we are under strain here together."

"She called me for you—so I thought."

"I asked her to." He walked to his bedroom door and shut it.

“My wife, she said you asked about a psychiatrist, one for me. But I don't need one.”

“She does?”

“Terribly.”

“Does she know it?”

“What has come our way won’t be easy Doctor. I'm not sure she can handle a storm such as this.”

“I’m not sure I can—”

“Doctor, my work is stressful. Not everybody is up to it, my wife is when all is well, but with arsonists burning down the church, and my despondency over that ungodly act, I'm not sure she can make it, without help I mean.”

“You need a recommendation?”

“Maybe two,” the pastor said.

She slept in the guest bedroom because sleeping in their bed with his constant movement would have denied her the little sleep she had sleeping alone. At first she responded to his calls, but after the third episode she surmised that he was not calling her, but fighting the fire in his dreams.

Early the next morning she woke and started to read before she noticed the quiet and she slipped into their bedroom and took a chair beside the bed. She was falling asleep when he turned over and the gun became visible.

On Sunday he conducted a service in a rented municipal office and said that he had put this savage act behind him, had forgiven the fugitive arsonists, and that he was intent that his church move on and put the matter behind them. He did not preach, except for incidental paraphrases of Scripture, but to the astonishment of listeners he laid out a plan to build a new church over the site of destruction. The congregation, which might have expected a rousing sermon on the vileness of human evil, or the tenacity of the human spirit, instead heard figures.

"What is he doing?" John whispered, turning to Edmond.

"I suspect he is trying to forget. What that man is going through is unimaginable. His work wouldn't do for the fainthearted," Edmond said.

"At least he doesn't have to contend with them anymore!" John quipped.

"Until they're caught," Edmond said, correcting him.

John might have talked more but the pastor started to speak again, though the congregation would be unwilling to move ahead with any plan for building soon, at least this early, but out of respect for their pastor, they did listen. The man had never been a man for numbers, but he threw them out like an accountant this day. His calculator lay on top of his Bible, and he used the two interchangeably as he made his case that the church must go on. A couple times his words worked despite tears, tears he explained as still seeping from his hurts, despite the extraordinary appearance he presented for a man who had just lost his church.

The town was small and there was one man who doubled as an investigator for the next town. His work took time, for the old church was sprawling and with the basement included three floors. Charred ruins lay everywhere, and he spent hours and then days, and after that weeks poking and pouring over every piece of the disaster. The pastor became outraged when the investigator could not tell him with any assurance when he might finish. The pastor's warning that the man would be impeding the work of God proved fruitless to move him.

Earlier depression returned for a day to the pastor and he confined himself at home again, but on Friday he resigned his membership in several community organizations as protest over the police obstruction of his building project.

Still more days passed with no news from the police on the search for the fugitives and in his sermon the next Sunday he compared Boger to Sodom and Gomorrah. With no hope in sight, the pastor soon escalated his protest by carrying a sign around his neck and picketing in front of the destroyed church. When he was told to get a permit for his exercise of free speech, he adamantly refused, and was jailed by the officers he now loathed for the creeping investigation.

He mocked the opportunity to make bail—even though several of his congregation stepped forward and offered wallets sufficient to cover that amount. Instead he brokered an agreement with the police, whereby he was allowed to assume his pulpit on Sunday mornings, but returned to his cell for the rest of the week. His flock, except for one hour on Sunday, would be without their shepherd. His wife protested his protesting, and threatened to leave him if he did not come out of his confinement, but this only made the pastor more adamant in his cry of injustice toward him and his church. The wife meanwhile refused to join his civil disobedience, but others of the congregation took to protesting on the street as he had done, and were jailed, as he had been, and some refused, as their shepherd did, to accept bail.

The sizeable endowment of the church made the pastor's idea of rebuilding not altogether unthinkable, and because the church would collect a substantial sum of money from their insurance policy, the congregation requited its earlier opposition to a seemingly hasty building project, and the new building was voted on the next Sunday and passed. Not a few of the votes were swayed by the courage of a pastor undeterred by his opponents, and his resilient faith that God would build his church. The pastor collapsed when the result of the ballots was announced, and he was carried out of the room for some minutes to compose himself, but he eventually returned and announced a celebration in his cell out of appreciation for the supportive congregation. An afternoon and part of an evening were improvised for fun and merriment, as the pastor who only days before had been unable to talk or move, was again his old self, and moved freely among most of his guests.

After the investigator located residual remains of three bodies in the basement of the destroyed church, the police were even more adamant that any construction wait and the pastor was livid. Now that his congregation had approved the building plan, the police had the unenviable position of stopping what was about to move forward, except for them. Dental records provided a match with the identity of the suspects, but the police investigator puzzled over the incompetence of arsonists who could not manage a fire without torching themselves. The pastor charged the police with more concern for the dead than the living, and provided a passage from Scripture to show how God is concerned for those on earth and in heaven, but not those under the earth.

Family members of the deceased were questioned, and some corroborated a story about a meeting the unfortunate three had attended the evening of the fire, but none of them could confirm its whereabouts or who had called the meeting.

"I knew one of them, Abe Abbot. He wasn't a complete stranger to me, I knew him, not well, but he lived a couple blocks from me. He acted odd, I mean that twitch he had and I saw him once in his back yard, praying on his knees—out loud."

"We can't put up with this forever," Edmond said to him as they slipped out of the congregation and away from the fight. They gaped in astonishment through the glass and Edmond even swore a little. John might have said something, but the man hurling castigations through the air made him shudder.

Edmond wiped his face and shook his head. "If we don't do something, we know what it will be next week, or the week after that."

The pastor lost his clerical patience and screamed at his accuser, but the accuser scurried from his seat and erased the distance between the two before the pastor turned to run. The man lunged toward the podium as the pastor tripped, but when the pastor's adversary got behind the podium and laid his open Bible on it, the pastor charged him shouting at the top of his lungs. For a while it looked like the antagonists would brawl.

"And then he said something worse. He said God is not here, because he's here," he said, and John pointed toward the podium.

"We'd better get back in there," Edmond shouted.

The pastor's face was swollen.

"I dismissed church," he said.

"Where's he at?" Edmond asked.

"Who?"

"The heckler!" Edmond said.

"He left," someone volunteered, but Edmond looked blank, and his face elicited more explanation from the Pastor, but he got none.

"Pastor they gotta go, no two ways about it," John said. The pastor's eyes fixed on Edmond, and no one said anything else until John asked the pastor what he thought they should do.

"I think we should all go home and pray. I suggest you all do the same. If you need to reach me you know where I'll be."

Bolstered by the courage of a pastor enduring interruptions of his sermons again, more members stepped forward to emulate his hardships, and more took up residence in the local jail with him. The pastor's salary was not jeopardized by his living situation, but for other parishioners who had employment outside the benefits of clergy, the decision to defer financial gratification for principle proved more excruciating. Relationships between fractured couples worsened, as became evident in that deteriorating union between the pastor and his wife, plus the pastor now had the extra task of counseling parishioners in prison over the merits of their decision to live in the jail and outside their households. Despite the enormous pain of households in strain, the pastor reminded them of Jesus' words that those who follow Him would become separated from those of their own household.

"Killer!" the heckler screamed and parishioners turned to see the prisoner, having tired of the heckling. A policeman on stage proceeded to remove the shackles his prisoner insisted upon wearing during transport from his cell.

"Killer," she shouted again, and this time she glared at the pulpit and the policemen who had positioned themselves around the man.

"It's amazing he has endured," Edmond said and John nodded.

"Don't know what his wife gets out of her protest," Edmond said, as the pastor rose to his podium.

5

The Daughter-in-Law

Quinton Strikeharder fell off Rockknob Hill backwards, shattering the bottle in his left hip pocket. The broken pieces cut as his body weight rolled downhill, and after slamming into a split boulder and a half hour of convulsing and thrashing about on wet ground, he finally bled to death. The New Testament his wife gave him three weeks earlier the undertaker found in Strikeharder's front pocket, spotted with blood and soaked in the wetness and smell of spirits. The undertaker called on the wife of the deceased and questioned why a drunk bothered to carry a Testament.

Susie Strikeharder said she would pick up anything of Quinton's, but when Quinton's mother Minnie heard about the accident, she ran to the new widow and urged her not to bother, before Minnie called on the undertaker and offered to pay for the burial. The older woman told her daughter-in-law she should never have married the good for nothing, as Minnie Strikeharder habitually referred to her youngest son. Minnie was headed out of town to see her sister up in the Cities, and curtly told the new widow and the undertaker before she left that Susie Strikeharder should count her blessings now that Quinton was dead.

"I told her what anybody woulda said. Honey this too will pass and it ain't much. He left you with nothing, because he was nothing to begin with. I know how that girl got mixed up with him—I ain't stupid. You know how they is; think they can change Satan, if 'n they a mind to, but she never did nothing with him, not the least thing. And no wonder. Most kids leave when they turn eighteen if their parents ain't done right by them. Him—him I couldn't dread purgatory after my time with him. Then he got up with her, her young and stupid, and him of no account, and she fell for him anyway, never mind me talking till I was blue in the face."

Minnie Strikeharder said all that before she had crossed the threshold of her sister's house, while Martha her sister stood flabbergasted, but asked her to come in anyway.

He had change in one front pocket, forty cents, and the Testament in the other. There was nothing else, at least not anything the undertaker produced. He told her Quinton's body would lie in a plot kept for those needing no ceremony for the hell awaiting them.

"Want a preacher?" he asked her, with little care for the tone of his question.

Susie Strikeharder didn't say much, and she said nothing now. She stood absorbed with thoughts about Quinton's soul more than anything about the corpse next to her. She had answers for the cruder questions, but she answered none and went back home after she identified the body and kissed the hard cheek before she left the building. Quinton's Testament she kept and carried in her bag, though it was sloping wet and reeked with the smell of alcohol. The small book she wrapped in newspaper the undertaker's cleaning man provided.

"That girl beat anything I ever seen," Minnie Strikeharder said to her sister. "Heaven knows I don't know what she saw in that good for nothing, but I wondered, after they's married, what he wanted with her. He never said that I knew, but she weren't like him, thank the Almighty. When he turned about thirteen he just started floating like a mindless river buoy, and I suspected then he'd not amount to much. Surprised me afterward he'd work at all, or that he could keep him and her up, but I guess he did. They never come to me for money, not that I'd give them any anyways. Maybe she did some trapping out in them woods for meat while he was gone off to work. I never did see a lot of victuals around that place. I's just glad at the time that she took him off my hands, though understand I weren't wishing him on nobody, and I tried my bestest to talk her away from him. I thanked the Almighty the minute I heard that He took the good for nothing off her hands. Maybe she'll show some gumption now."

Susie couldn't sleep her first widowed night, and two hours after midnight she got up and placed the couple's framed picture from the dresser on Quinton's pillow in their bed. Quinton had little expression on his face, but he was holding her hand in the picture, and he did have on a shirt and tie. They had the picture made one week after marrying, and she kept it first on the mantle in their main room and then on the top of a secretly borrowed dresser from her sister.

The bed she lay in alone he always took care of in the mornings. Susie got up with Quinton on the days he worked and she cooked him breakfast, and while she did he remade the bed and then got dressed. Neither task took him long, and he would walk into the kitchen and sit at the table until the food was ready, and then they would have their meal together after she said grace.

He never complained that Susie remembered, and for her that meant Quinton Strikeharder had managed to change one thing about his life, maybe because that was nearly all his mother did.

The first time they visited her after the wedding, Minnie Strikeharder laid into Quinton about his drinking, and after they left he asked Susie if she wanted to go back sometime. She said they should, but Quinton just shook his head as if to say no, and the subject never came up again and they never visited again. They endured her visits when the woman made her rounds and ranted at her son without invitation, calling him good for nothing, and without fail she told Susie what a mistake the girl had made marrying him. Usually Quinton would escape outside if the weather was decent—when he was not too intoxicated—while the two women stayed inside, and the elder woman would talk down Quinton to Susie.

"I once tried to reason with him, when he was younger. Done no good. He sat staring at me with nearly closed eyes and a body practically falling over from drinking. He weren't like his brothers, no not a bit like 'em. His brothers done something with themselves, and they had dabbled with that bottle too, like their pappy, but when they saw what it did, how it killed him, they ran from that drinking like it was Satan himself. The good for nothing, he was too young to see much of that, so when he started drinking there was nothing to stop him or break him. I told him his daddy could have been sitting in the chair beside him that day if'n he had laid off the liquor, but he didn't hear me, couldn't, passed out before I's finished. And then that crazed girl shows up and gets him to marry. Least she got him off me, that I'll give her credit for." Minnie paused, as Martha looked on, and then Minnie took more tea.

Susie fell asleep after the sun came up at six and slept until noon. She felt no appetite for food, but she wandered toward the tiny kitchen anyway and spotted Quinton's Testament on the bureau, in the decorative plate they got for a wedding present from Susie's sister.

Susie had given the Testament to Quinton three weeks earlier. She presented it to him before, three times, but she found it in the trash every time. When she saw the print of the book in his front pocket after her fourth attempt, she resisted asking questions and started to pray.

She pulled the book closer, as the faint smell of spirits wafted toward her nostrils. The spine and pages had dried in the stifling heat of the house, and now every page lay warped and stiff between the covers.

Quinton was private and hardly talked, even when you talked to him. He talked more before they married, and his "I do" seemed almost the last significant interaction she had with him besides intercourse. She reckoned after a while Quinton must be depressed real bad. He rarely smiled, and he showed no difference around children, even very small ones. She figured then her dream of having children must go, knowing that they should not be in this marriage.

He went to work most every day, except those days that he had too much to drink the day before. On such days, he mostly lay in bed. If it was nice weather, he might stumble outside and sit in the sun, usually on the ground, and rarely in the one outside chair they owned. She would walk out sometimes just to be with him, but she usually never asked him if he wanted to talk because then he might say nothing. Little about Quinton seemed to change, except for the fact that he had kept the Testament for three weeks, and he didn't complain like his mother.

"Yep, Jack and Shepherd did something with themselves, but the good for nothing--he never did. I was hoping she could do something with him, but she couldn't, and the only good thing he ever did for her was dying. I hope she'll use her chance now. I ain't gonna say I'm expecting much though."

Minnie reached for a cookie from the plate that her sister had laid on the table.

Susie's eyes moistened after she saw Quinton's name scribbled in the front of the Testament.

She rarely saw Quinton read or write, though she knew he could. She never had a letter written in his hand, because they had lived close enough before marrying to converse in person, but he had made his signature on their marriage documents, because she did everything to accord with the laws of God and man. She rubbed her finger over the letters in Quinton's name. That last name—Strikeharder—it had frightened her at first, until she met Quinton.

Though Quinton hardly talked, Susie Strikeharder never reasoned that it was her. She partly surmised she had put the man to thinking and that when Quinton was thinking he didn't talk. She had seen in his eyes that he wanted something, but she refrained from badgering him. She thought that one day he would simply open up and talk incessantly. If that never happened, she prayed he might at least talk to God.

She turned to the Testament's inside back cover. Quinton's name stood there, printed handsomely and upright, almost proudly, like he wanted to make sure his name stayed permanently in the book. She was never sure if Quinton's ears worked more than his tongue, and she had doubted if what she said to him went in or stayed out.

She rubbed her finger over his name and started to weep.

"How did he appear to you?"

"Himself."

"And how was that?"

"He was standing behind me."

"Did anybody else see him?"

"Don't anybody live there but me."

"Nobody saw him?"

"I saw him."

"No one else?"

"Not unless he showd himself to them."

"Did he say anything?"

"His face did."

"What?"

"He saw hell—where he could a gone."

"What did hell say to him?"

"Hell don't talk to ya, its torment."

"What kind of torment?"

"Separation from God."

"Can he adapt there?"

"Adapt?"

"Did he want to go there?"

"Nobody wants to go there."

"What did it look like?"

"Hell."

"He didn't like it there?"

"Don't nobody like it there."

"Why does anybody go?"

"You don't go. You get sent."

"Do you think he'll be going back, I mean to see it again?"

"No, he got snatched back."

"Does he regret that?"

"Regret?"

"Will he miss seeing it?"

"Don't nobody miss it."

Dear Martha,

I said I'd let you know how things was when I got back down here, and I'm keepin my promise. I'm sorry she interrupted my visit like that—I guess I made the mistake telling her before I left where I was going. And so she musta told them. Anyways, that's what they said when I got back down her. She's got nobody here that bothers with her. When she married the good for nothing, her whole family so far as I know, because they knowd better than she did about him, disowned her, for marrying his kind. They knowd better than her, but she kept saying to them that all things was possible with God. I had told her before, and then her family told her, that she weren't God. But she wouldn't listen.

Near as I can tell, she's not listening to any of them doctors either, least none that has talked to me. I'm still not figuring how they got her, or if she's got them because they can't make heads ner tails of her. I laughed. I told em, join the crowd. They ask me where she came from, and I told them just down the road from my place, but they just look at me stupid. I guess they not used to a lot of variety.

Course with what she may have told them and all, don't know that I'd not be wondering about her too. She better give up thinking about him and listen. He's past and she better forget him. I told her that when I left to come up there. You better move on I said, but I expect she ain't for a while. She never would listen to anybody, like I told you.

Your sister,
Minnie Strikeharder

"Is he in your dreams?"

"He ain't in my dreams."

"Where is he?"

"In heaven."

"Heaven?"

"Heaven."

"Where's that?"

"Where you want to be after you die."

"Does he see God?"

"God sees him. And everything else."

"How does God see everything?"

"He might tell you, if you really wanting to know."

"Do you ever ask God anything?"

"I asked Him right before I saw Quinton, why he took Quinton."

"What did he say?"

"He didn't say. I turned around and I saw Quinton."

"Which do you love most?"

"What you mean?"

"God or Quinton?"

"The Good Book says you to love God with all your heart mind and soul, and that daughter-in-law and mother-in-law may not be at peace because of Christ."

"Did Quinton come between you and God?"

"God brought Quinton to me. Ain't nothing right in what you say."

Dear Martha,

They's talking about puttin her away. I mean just lettin her be and quit trying to talk sense to her. Just shut her up someres and let her talk herself hoarse. It don't appear to me that they knocking even a dent in her. I told um you couldn't tell this girl anything, and when I said that, they wanted to talk to me more. I reckoned they figured I might clue them or something. She does seem happy, and heaven knows she oughta be, she got rid of him. I never seen her quite like this with him. Before she's just composed. Maybe I was looking at him too much.

Your sister,

Minnie Strikeharder

"With your husband dead, you'll want to get on with your life."

"He was dead. I got no worry now."

"Will he be with you now?"

"He's with God."

"Who will be with you?"

"God. He's always been with me, since I was little."

"But your big now."

"God's bigger."

"Maybe you should think less about God."

"God came to me long time ago, saved me. You don't forget nothing like that."

"But God took Quinton."

"I thanked God for what Christ did for Quinton."

"Quinton's gone now."

"God gives and He takes. Don't call God to account. That's backwards."

"He took your husband."

"He did. Someday He'll take you."

Dear Martha,

Pardon my putting off writing to you. I'm hoping you'll get down here to see me soon, soon as things settle down some more here. They really don't much need more settlin though, that's taken care of mostly. It's the newness of the whole thing. I ask her to come here cause the girl for all her ways was right for him, and I think she's tryin again. She went over to her peoples, and near as I know, made her amends with em. As you know, her family was mostly put off because they didn't want her marrying the likes of him. I'm wishin now I could take back some things, but I'm not gonna be frettin anymore like I was for a few days when she first come. Truth is I wouldn't felt anything if it weren't for her. You know how I felt about Quinton. Seems they couldn't get her to stop over at that place they was keepin her. She didn't ask me to come here. I ask her to come, mostly not for any pity for her, cause the girls got more than I'd gave her credit for. I ask her here cause I'm grateful now. You mayna never heard such as this outa me, but I am.

Your sister,

Minnie Strikeharder

6

Arrogance

"Nothing comes between us and Him," James continued, as he smacked his lips. "When we meet Him, there'll be nothing between us and Him. Just our lonesome." James eased back into the seat he had to himself, while Jane and her husband Paul tasted their sandwiches in the front.

"We knew you liked them," Jane said, smiling at James, and she handed him the second sardine sandwich that fell into his mouth after he rolled up the two squares of bread.

"You know He once had a fish fry without going fishing," James said, as Jane and Paul finished their first bites.

"I wish I could get you two to come, I mean just give it a try. We got nothing fancy; no crosses mind you, and none of those pretties that distract you from Him."

The two in the front remained silent, with effort.

"I got Him in my heart, not hanging on my chest," he said, as the two people in the front seat worked at the virtue of patience. Jane pointed to the orange lilies in the side ditch.

"I gave up the pretties when I got Him. He asked for it all, and I gave it to Him."

Paul grimaced.

"Truth is, I don't care anything about these gardens we're going to, but I couldn't turn down an invitation from you. Couldn't we just pull over for a minute before we get there and I could pray for you, and then we could go on about your pretties?"

"But then we wouldn't have any interest in them," Paul said.

"Things of this world, you're right my friend," James said. "Why if you're in His care, that's the best kind of care. I mean there's a blanket of prayer around this car right now, because I asked for it after you nice folks invited me yesterday. I don't go anywhere without it."

Jane clutched her crucifix and remained silent while her husband mumbled.

James sat comfortably basking in the soft backseat before the monstrous truck bumper tore into his flesh. The thick steel sheared the gas tank and slammed his slight figure forward between the other two. The savage impact smashed the trapped bodies caught inside the crunching metal before each was escorted out of the blazing heap.

An attendant came with ear plugs and blindfolds.

When anyone reached the table, other attendants in charge of collecting the mercy tokens required their return, and Paul spotted one figure pleading and then fighting to keep the devices to delay the imminent horror ahead, with dire consequence. The disobedient figure persisted fruitlessly, while the attendant methodically bound the screaming human and then effortlessly stripped him for the table. Tears produced scalding on the reddened face while quivering figures behind the futile resistor plummeted to their knees and kneaded hard at their faces.

James hid his swollen head between his knees to countenance his eyes. Paul mercifully went ahead of him—stepped in front—and James screeched his thanks. He had had no voice for the past hour.

Few minutes remained for them before the table of judgment would send them to separated worlds. Attendants mandated ten paces between the individuals lined up for miles before eternity, but Paul closed the ten paces to assist James with the tokens of mercy. Some took the ear plugs and blindfolds while some refused or took one but not the other. James asked for both, but his tiny hands shook too much to get either item in the right place. The attendant snatched them off the ground and escorted Paul back to his position.

Some reckonings scarcely took any time, but usually ended violently when guards bound the damned for their journey. Others managed miniscule delaying tactics before the final verdict, but never long nor enough. Everybody got the same questions and questions came in advance.

Paul had one of the few souls James' limited vision beheld lacking wounds, portend for the new body promised for the rewarded, and he saw guards treating the sheep and goats accordingly; the judgment table stood as a final formality of guilt or innocence, redemption or damnation.

Some of the figures swapped vulgarities about their eroding bodily estate; the farsighted grieved gargantuan remorse for their imperiled souls. A few sprouted fouled money protruding from their emaciated forms and used it for coveted positions further from the invincible table of judgment. Still others, resigned to a fate unthinkable, would not think just yet, and instead blithely frolicked and relished their last pleasures, ignoring the final judgment and dark eternity ahead. Some guzzled drink and some had arms around the bellies and chests of companions. Most nearest the table gyrated frantically to sell themselves for delayed position further back in line.

The sheer noise of shrieks and wails proved deafening so near the front, and Paul requested ear plugs on the remote chance he could converse with James from such distance, though soon nobody heard anything save the horrific sound of gasping breaths from the condemned. Vision began to fail, though James heard some distant voices ahead, singing songs to their Redeemer.

Paul ventured backward to bring James forward after the attendant signaled for the line to move again, though James refused to go, so the attendant snatched the closest limb and drug James' flailing flesh face down across mountains of refuse. The large head snagged in the rubble, and the attendant motioned for needed assistance. Two attendants tried to separate the head that James's spindly arms hung onto, and then three attendants, but they too proved no match for a mind now determined to take itself elsewhere, so instead they bound his limbs and stripped him. No resistor ever succeeded. Paul was escorted back to his position by an attendant, never close enough that he would hold James' hand again.

The one behind the left table had stood up to view the commotion, applauded the rebellious spirit, and it smiled at James. James returned the gesture until his failing vision determined that the odiferous face genuflecting before him had welcomed him. He wanted to scream at the gruesome laughter, but he had no voice.

With no benefit for remorse possible this close to final judgment, he searched frantically over his shoulder for a trade like the rest of the imminently damned, but the damned mocked when they saw his offer. One spit on him and some jeered, but none courted him. He swung around after his shoulder was tapped, hopeful of some negotiation, but the teaser kicked him in the stomach and the slumping figure spewed undigested sardines across a surface littered with every idol imaginable.

Paul stood at the right table. With his stare fixed on Jane, he surmised she must have passed through first.

7

Wise as Serpents

The candidate wailed, waiting for Zenu outside an office door where the huge "Believe" sign hung conspicuously. Zenu cast an expectant eye to see if the candidate saw it, but there was no such luck. The prostrate figure had bulging red eyes producing a pool of wet splatters on the oak floor and Zenu motioned for his secretary while he cradled the grieving man and drug him onto a red couch in a corner of the office. His clothes were rumpled and ill fitted to a body that could have done with less shirt and more trouser. He had the appearance of someone from the stage and Zenu recalled how many of them came to him after they pretended to be something they were not.

"How did he get here?" he asked the mop handler.

"He was at the front door when I got here this morning," she said.

"No papers, no identification?"

"Nothing but a crucifix around his neck."

"We better get if off. He may hang himself with it," Zenu said, shaking his head, and telling Greta that good intentions guaranteed nothing and often lead to disaster

"He seems anxious. You should try to talk to him," she said.

Greta was the most intelligent of Zenu's staff, but she could not do his work for him, though she caused him the least irritation of any of his staff. Zenu pulled up a chair beside the man to hold a shaking hand, while Greta stepped back to her office.

"Tell me how Arthur is doing," Zenu instructed when another staff member entered the office.

"He was uneasy, but the rest has been good, and he has his faculties again," John answered.

John expected more questions, but he knew better than to speak out of turn. Zenu seldom made eye contact with his employees, except when he gave orders and John now fiddled with his clipboard while he waited for anything more. Zenu looked irritated at the noise. The staff viewed small obstacles as mountains, though he showed them time and again every reason to take the opposite view.

"This sort of thing disturbs me. When was he here last?" Zenu asked in staccato fashion, and John pulled the clipboard up from his side while his eyes shaded toward Zenu.

"That was twelve days ago, Father. Arthur was here for three days."

"Can you tell me about it?" Zenu began with the candidate, extraordinarily competent at doing two things at once. He always began with that question with the new ones, but the candidate shrieked and rose up and struck Zenu's face. The sweaty hand slapped Zenu's face again and Greta burst into the room, knocking over Zenu's tall floor lamp before she sandwiched herself between the two bodies. She grabbed at the man's shoulders to force him back down on the couch, while Zenu fell backwards.

Zenu relaxed because he was tired. He had never dreamed that his star pupil Arthur might not be a pupil of his, but when the pupil returned, Zenu had started to question his effectiveness and silently thought he might be losing a touch he had once had that could heal virtually any and all aspirants that came to him. Arthur was different, Zen knew that it the beginning, but it had worked in favor of their relationship at the start, and through it, as Zenu thought the Arthur might in time be more than just a student of his. When the student returned, now a second time, he had just cause to worry not just about Arthur, but himself.

Zenu did not know if harm was intended because novices sometimes mistook him for someone in their past, and he reminded himself of that now. After Greta forced the body flat on the couch, Zenu thought he heard the man laugh, but grieving candidates often exuded tears or laughter that meant the same thing. While the man was still pinned, Zenu reached down and jerked the crucifix off. Zenu frowned as he dangled the ornament in front of the wet face. The eyes of the man welled up and his body grew limp from Greta's hold.

"Shall we try again?" Zenu asked, as Greta stepped away, and he sat down and held the hand again. The prone body spewed something garbled that Zenu could not understand, and Zenu reached over to rub the man's moist forehead.

Zenu had been the founder and director of the Center for five years with a string of unbroken successes. He delighted in his work, and he expected it to work all the time. He put everyone who came to the Center under a strict regimen of studying his books and papers and if they needed more instruction, he presented them with other literature of the tradition. His intellectual resources were without limit, and he never worried because of it.

"Is Arthur up to visitors?" he asked John.

"I think so. There are reports that he called for your books and was reading again," John said.

"That's a good sign. Arrange for me to visit him in thirty minutes. I don't need much more than ten or so minutes should do. No, pencil in five minutes. I shall be surprised if it takes any more than that," Zenu concluded, and John spouted something about the brilliance of his boss and left.

The candidate exhaled a breath that Greta heard from her desk.

"All the things you have heard—it is much worse. I mean . . . look at me!" and the man began sobbing before his words to Zenu were finished.

Zenu rubbed the forehead as he held the clammy hand. The story was too familiar to him. He had seen countless young men come to him broken and begging for help, but with little hope left. He often wondered how these crushed spirits managed enough strength to cry for aid.

"I fear I may never be normal again, even with your help. I may need extra time," the candidate added, and he removed his arm from across his face and gazed at the ceiling. The visitor began to recount some of the horrors he had lived through, but Zenu placed a gentle but firm hand over his visitor's mouth when the words became unintelligible. The face on the prone body trembled until Zenu started to explain.

"No horror you can tell could surpass the horror of those living within these walls. The demonic has been everywhere and done everything. There is no new thing it can do," he said, as he turned to his window to focus attention outside at the library where students sat at study in the window cubicles. Every head was bowed over a book and only rarely did anyone look up from their study. Zenu directed the man's eyes to the composure of these learners and the visitor's eyes started to show some dryness for the first time.

"But Father, can I call you Father?"

"Yes, of course, I want you to."

"Can you help me? I know there have been others, but—"

"We shall begin to process you in this morning and—"

Zenu jumped when the phone rang.

"I shall visit you again in your quarters once you have settled in," he said to his newest novice. The novice managed a faint smile, while Zenu's secretary walked into his office. Zenu frowned at her.

"I asked you to defer all calls," Zenu said to Greta.

"It's the librarian. He insists it cannot wait. Someone has requested to see the banned books," she said, as she walked back to her desk.

"Who made this request?" Zenu demanded.

"You can see for yourself. He is sitting right over there." The librarian waved a hand toward the corner table.

"And what is he doing there?" Zenu demanded again.

"You can ask him. He is sitting right over there." The librarian smiled with an expression Zenu had come to despise over the past months, but the librarian's belligerence was trumped by the false report on Arthur that Zenu had received from John minutes earlier. "Idiots," he muttered to himself as he walked toward Arthur.

"I had not expected to see you so soon," Zenu said, as he worked to disguise his surprise with an insincere smile.

Arthur looked up but returned to his book. Zenu stood and looked around before he pulled out a chair from the table. He sat down and Arthur grunted as he moved his finger across the text.

"How are you?" Zenu asked.

Arthur looked up but went back to his book again.

"Arthur, can I help you?" Zenu asked.

Arthur kept his finger on his text as he looked around the library and then at the librarian.

"Arthur, what is it?" Zenu asked, and he etched his chair closer to his former student.

Zenu feared that Arthur was worse than he had imagined. Arthur's face had a tepid smile and he made a soft grunting sound as his finger moved under the lines on his page.

“Arthur, what is it?” Zenu asked again.

“It's God,” Arthur said.

“God?” Zenu asked, in shock, and then he remained silent for some seconds. He tried to control his anger, but his face had reddened before the solitary syllable left his tongue. He looked hard at Arthur.

“God,” Arthur said again, but this time with more feeling.

“There is no God!” Zenu said and he stood up from his chair. Arthur made his grunting sound again and Zenu went to confer with the librarian.

“How long has he been here?” Zenu demanded.

The librarian checked the log.

“One hour,” he answered.

“What book does he have?” Zenu continued.

“You didn't see it?”

“No.”

“It is one of your books,” the librarian said.

“Did he request a title from the banned books?”

“No, he only requested to see them.”

Zenu walked back to Arthur's table and sat down, though he would prefer to grab Arthur’s shoulders and shake him. Arthur turned his book over and folded his hands on the table.

“What is it Arthur?”

“It's God. You lost God.”

“No Arthur. We never found him, remember. We never found him because he's not there to find.” Zenu stood up.

Arthur sat still.

When the librarian called the next day Zenu called the librarian to his office, before going out to see Arthur again. The librarian arrived ten minutes for Zenu, who was now walking in circles with the lamp still on the floor from the previous day. Zenu never noticed such things, and Greta did not seem to mind, but she did walk in when the librarian arrived to set the lamp back upright.

"I don't know if you have any suggestions on how to handle this matter, but I'm willing to entertain any," Zenu said as he motioned for the librarian to take a seat on the couch. The librarian looked straight at Zenu, but he said nothing, and Zenu stared back at him, resolved not to speak until the librarian had something to offer.

"I don't think there is anything you can do," the librarian said when Zenu practically threatened him for a suggestion after five minutes of silence.

"What does that mean?" Zenu asked.

"The man is happy," the librarian responded.

Zenu's face flushed and he stood up.

"The man has lost his reason you fool!"

The librarian was about to comment further, but Zenu stormed out and the librarian would follow him to the library, but not before he stopped to chat with Greta.

"Arthur you have requested to see the banned books—twice now. Why do you want to see them?" Zenu asked.

Arthur held up an index finger for Zenu to wait while he finished his sentence. Arthur scribbled on his paper and folded his hands on the table.

"You have come here again because you need help. Now you've got to let me help you," Zenu said.

"You lost God," Arthur said.

"Arthur there is no God!! Have you lost everything I taught you?"

"You forgot where you put Him," Arthur said.

"Arthur I didn't put him anywhere, because he's nowhere to put!" Zenu said.

"You forgot where you put Him," Arthur repeated.

"Arthur, listen to me!" Zenu lunged up from his chair as the librarian peered in their direction.

"You lost God," Arthur repeated.

"Arthur what is this?" Zenu's face was turning from red to white. "Arthur you have got to let me help you!" Zenu shouted this time, but Arthur began writing again.

Zenu walked away from the table and swore under his breath, out of earshot of Arthur as he tugged at his shirt. He found a window and rested his forehead on the cool glass. The blood vessels in his head throbbed and he reached out to the wall to steady himself. A chair next to the window was empty and he sat down before John stepped into the library. Arthur was different this time and Zenu knew it. He seemed ready to taunt rather than just question, something he had never done before. Zenu liked the old Arthur better.

John's eyes fastened on Zenu when he came in, but Zenu did not move, nor did he converse with John as his eyes fixed on the floor.

"That will do," John said to Arthur, loud enough for Zenu to hear. "You have gravely disappointed your mentor." The two smiled at one another, as Zenu returned, but he called John to his office and let Arthur be for now.

Zenu shook his head, and looked at John and then at the floor. He squinted his eyes and settled back in his chair, rubbing his small hands through thinning hair, as he starred at the shelves in his office. The abundance of plaques on his walls left little wall space and he counted all of them as he contemplated his first failure. His tired eyes skipped to the library he could see out of his window. Arthur was visible in one of the window cubicles and Zenu recalled brighter days when Arthur had first come. He had been so impressive and such a sponge that Zenu had dreamed in those days that Arthur might someday take his own place as director at the Center.

That dream had never left him, despite Arthur's situation now. Arthur of course had forgotten the awfulness of his condition when he first came to the Center, and Zenu's reminders of it to him would probably be without effect he thought.

Zenu was tired. Too tired for something that took too much thinking.

And then it came. Arthur needed the novice! Oh providence in a world without it! Oh a world where believers were the best obstacle to belief!! Arthur would see himself in the novice, and still too the novice would see the fixed Arthur. The two were blind, and he with make them both see, by seeing each other. How could he have missed that? Experience is the best teacher, and he would use it now.

"I can fix Arthur with the novice; no, no, I can fix both of them," he shouted, and then he screamed. Zenu's eyes opened wide and his face shone like that of an angel. He jumped up from his chair and romped through his office, and he knocked the lamp down again before John moved to a corner of the room. Zenu began to rake his slight hand through the thinning hair as his pace quickened.

Greta came to the door.

"Is something wrong," she asked, looking at a lamp on the floor twice in one week.

"No, and no," he said. "Something is right," and he lunged to hug his secretary, something no one recalled him doing before.

"Come with me," Zenu ordered John, as he raced out the door. John lingered with Greta after Zenu was gone but when he reached the library, he kept his distance while Zenu approached Arthur's table like a hunter who already has one slug in an injured animal. Zenu strutted to the table with all the pomp of a regal function.

"Arthur I think it is time you were permitted to look at the banned books," Zenu said.

Arthur looked up, but he had no expression that Zenu could see.

"Yes, it is time," Zenu said again and a smile spread over a face that had been contorted only minutes earlier.

"Father, I am not so sure that this is for the best," John interjected.

Zenu turned around.

"I'll handle this!" he said curtly to John, as Zenu contemplated more details of the plan that his mind had been fabricating, and a plan was sorely needed, for the new novice had made no progress after his first three days. Zenu, distracted by Arthur more each day, had done nothing about him. The screams of the novice made sleep and study for other members erratic at best and Zenu had started to fear disruption to the community. He had tried to talk to the novice, but the novice's calm lasted only as long as Zenu talked to him. When the novice was alone again his screams intensified, and usually started the minute Zenu walked out of his cell. Zenu knew that a cellmate might stop the screaming, but this sacrifice—if it meant him—was out of the question.

"Before I permit you use of the books Arthur, you must earn them. I want you to help me with a young novice who has recently come to our community, and I want you to stay with him for a time," Zenu said, as he continued to smile at Arthur. Zenu had a little speech planned, but Arthur asked for the room number of the young novice and grabbed his belongings to leave.

"Wait a minute Arthur!" Zenu said, and he held his hand up like a policeman stopping traffic.

"Arthur I do not expect thanks now, but I will later, when you will find yourself in my flock again."

"Am I dismissed?" Arthur asked, like a schoolboy mocking the pretension he begrudges from an inferior.

The screams coming from the novice lasted all night, but when the sun rose they diminished, and stopped altogether a half hour later. Zenu had anticipated that possibility in the beginning, but the intolerable night did not sit well with the rest of the community who had had virtually no sleep at all and with the screams they complained to John minutes after

Zenu was gone. Zenu had announced that he would take off for two days to reward himself for his solution.

Arthur and the novice came out of the cell at noon to confer with John in Zenu's office.

When Zenu returned for work two days later, he was eager to know the current condition of his project.

"It's too early to tell yet Father," John cautioned in answer to the barrage of questions from Zenu. Zenu peppered John with more questions, and John cautioned him again from expecting too much too soon.

"Yes, of course, and I should just leave them alone," he said.

Zenu could not leave them alone, so before he started for the dormitory the next morning to see the current state of his project, Greta stopped him.

"For you," and she handed the phone to him.

Zenu did not stop by the librarian's desk but marched straight to the table where Arthur was sitting.

"You and I had an agreement!" Zenu protested.

"And I want my books," Arthur replied.

"Where's the novice?" Zenu demanded.

"There," and Arthur pointed to a desk in another corner of the library, as he went back to his reading.

"What have you done to him?" Zenu demanded.

"He's studying your book." Arthur said.

"What have you done to him?" Zenu demanded again. This time Zenu heard the novice making a grunting sound as he read and Zenu's face flushed with blood before it turned white.

"Get him back to his cell now!" Zenu ordered.

"I want my books Zenu," Arthur said, and Zenu grimaced at being addressed without his title.

His face stiffened and he expelled a voluminous breath through his nostrils. He grabbed the end of the table and pinched the oak desk top until his knuckles whitened and then he ordered Arthur off Center property.

Zenu had to sleep sometime, so he designated John to be in charge of the community during the day, while Zenu tried everything he could to calm the novice by night. Each morning John went to the novice's quarters for a decision from Zenu on whether a day off would be granted to the community for their sleep loss and Zenu grudgingly granted permission almost every other day, while he went home to sleep only to return by early evening for another night of screams with the novice. After Zenu left each morning Brother John put out a memo that everyone could rest until four in the afternoon, though at four thirty all community members would go to the library where the novice would lecture on sacred literature a half hour before dinner.

After two weeks of night duty and no noticeable improvement in the novice, Zenu's weariness started to show.

"I cannot devote all my time to him and neglect the rest of the community. Heaven knows in what kind of state they are. You know that every one of them is vulnerable," he said.

"This is true Father," John responded.

"The novice did tell me when he came that he did not know if I could help him. And perhaps he was right. But

John I cannot stomach a second lost soul, not after I have lost Arthur. That would be difficult, and it might do me in."

The novice made his loudest and longest screams that night, and before sunrise Zenu came out of the cell without stopping or conferring with John and walked to his vehicle and went home.

When Zenu left, the novice walked into Zenu's office where John offered the red-eyed man a fresh cup of coffee. Greta and the librarian joined them and poured coffee for themselves.

"I expect to finish moving the books today," the librarian said as he leaned against the wall of books. The four of them finished their coffee and began to sing.

That evening Zenu came without his night bag.

"I think this is it John," he said.

"What do you mean Father?" John asked.

"I think I must let the novice go. He was right, I cannot help him," he said and Zenu starred at the floor.

"I have not helped him," he said, and a small tear appeared from one eye.

The sound of music interrupted the moment of sorrow.

"What is that?" Zenu asked, with genuine surprise.

John looked at Zenu, but he would wait for Zenu to answer his own question. Zenu looked at his watch and then at John.

"It's almost meal time. Everyone should be in dining hall. Perhaps they are singing 'Death to God' before the meal," and a twinkle appeared in the eye that had seconds earlier produced a tear.

He halted at the library door after his ears made out the words, and he stood and gawked at community members stumbling through the hymn. He spotted two of his community close to the librarian's desk with their mouths pulled tight as if refusing to sing, and he held out hope as he stomped through the library, shoving bodies out of his way as he lurched toward the librarian's desk.

He held his hands over his ears, for the music crescendo as he approached the desk, and he swore at the off-key librarian, but the librarian held up a finger for Zenu to wait while he finished a solo part in the hymn. Zenu did not wait because he never waited and he lunged across the desk at the librarian, but two arms grasped his upper body from behind and held him in mid-air as his legs kicked.

"These two have requested to see some books," the librarian offered as he turned to address the suspended body of Zenu. Zenu's face turned white and a litany of profanities spewed from his mouth before he raised his legs and kicked the two petitioners in front of him. One of them bowled over from the blow to his chest, but the other stood shaken in disbelief.

"But Father, they are your books," he shouted as he pointed to the shelf behind the smiling librarian.

Zenu saw his books sitting on the shelf, but the singing smothered his curses.

8

Parental Grief

He had the foot caught in his mouth for three days--or so they said--and his parents called his brothers in after a week of it.

"Maybe the boy hasn't got all the intricacies of yoga down yet," Stan said to his brother Brady, and the two laughed.

"I'll bet the fool is dead before we get there," Brady replied, as he looked at his watch. They drove on the road for an hour before the sun came up, and still had breakfast yet to eat. The country between them and their destination looked less habitated than the time of their youth, and every passing chance to eat somewhere appeared bleaker than the place before.

"We may have to view the body on an empty stomach," Brady said, and Stan nodded. The two were not happy about such an interruption to their lives, but conceded to come anyway after their mom pleaded that their baby brother Josiah might not live through the day. They had never been close to him--he was their junior--but years alone did not discredit their own flesh and blood.

The boy grew up a rebel, and he had made his mom and dad suffer tremendously. The twins--Stan and Brady--told their parents to kick him out, "put his craziness onto his feet," as they said to their parents, repeatedly. Isabel and Frank did nothing, and Josiah did next to nothing.

On his sixteenth birthday he was in church because his parents insisted, and he had gone down the church aisle after the pastor's invitation, to his parent's exhilaration, but then he grabbed the robed cleric only to tell the congregation and the cleric that their shepherd was destined for hell for propagating lies. Isabel and Frank couldn't manage church for a year after that, and Josiah never went back, and nobody asked him back.

No prodding by his brothers could get Isabel and Frank to shove the boy out of their house, but Josiah went anyway, after a while, though he only managed a thousand feet of distance from his ancestral home.

He built a shack in the wood edge, not large nor long enough for him to lay his slim tall frame out, but that did not matter by then, because Josiah was spending most of his time in the sitting position meditating. Isabel and Frank would slip up quietly and stare through the plank cracks and observe their youngest sitting upright and as still as if he were dead. He quit coming to their house for food soon after the building was finished, surviving, they thought, on twigs and various leaf soups that he made. He was not far enough away from his parents for his older brothers.

"Maybe some of those mushrooms locked up his nervous system," Stan said to Brady, and they laughed again, before returning to conversation on the best stocks to squeeze for the fall quarter.

Josiah had few friends, no job that his parents could detect, and he sometimes had run-ins with the law. He had spent a night and on occasion a string of days in jail, though usually for some trivial offense, like indecent exposure when he sat meditating in the snow naked in front of a house whose owners Josiah disliked. His brothers told their parents in desperation that the boy needed counseling for such behavior, but Isabel and Frank had more faith in Josiah than they did counseling. After that, the two sons told their parents not to call them again--they had done their part, they said.

"Old place looks worse than ever," Brady said to Stan, and Stan looked up.

"No grass mowed. I guess we did it last," Stan said.

Stan pointed to the shack. "Reckon he's in there?"

"Course not, place is too small for theater. The dying deserve more atmosphere for the audience. Mom and Dad got him in the house where they can attend to his rotten condition."

"It don't look pretty."

"Nothing here ever was."

An ambulance sat parked in the yard, but with no evident activity, and the sheriff's car sat next to the oak tree beside the ambulance. The fescue in the yard came up to mid-point on the tires.

"I don't think I can stomach this," Brady said.

"What you mean?"

"He's got his theatrics going in there, no doubt."

"You're right. We told them to keep us out of this after all. We did our part."

The two sat still for another minute and started to leave when they heard a scuffle in the house and then a shot before they heard a crash.

The two jumped out of the Mercedes, but the sheriff and deputy's drawn guns met Brady and Stan as the two came up onto the porch. Josiah stood behind the officers.

"They should go easy. Not the violent type. White-collar criminals frown on it," Josiah said to the sheriff, smiling.

His brothers started to swear, but Josiah raised his hand.

"Sorry for the agitation in the house. Sheriff and me thought you two was about to hightail it out of here--so we had to prick your interest with a little commotion. Oh, and I will be visiting you in prison. That is, if they don't execute for crimes such as yours. Mine seem minuscule after what you two been up to."

Brady turned to Stan who was about to explode, and told his twin to keep quiet until their lawyer showed up. The sheriff and deputy handcuffed both and took them to the car, and their brother went back to his shack. The parent's cries could be heard through the windows.

9

Last Race

"She's fast is she?" James Dianio asked.

"Faster than your mouth!" Joe Sims answered, with little realization before tonight that he could marshal command of such company. The pack of youngsters followed the leader until another usurped the leader's place.

The crowd would normally fall at Dianio's feet before tonight, but they roared with laughter at Sims's retort, though Dianio didn't take tease, and he would not tolerate this upstart Sims. He'd teach the twerp a lesson and keep this pack obedient.

Joe Sims thought different and took the group's amusement to mean they had tired of Dianio, though Sims knew Dianio never let go easily. Sims had pondered Dianio in his mind awake and asleep for two years.

"Bout time for the twerp to chirp," James Dianio touted, and Sims knew that meant work for him, as well as opportunity.

Sims knew the group's rogue routine and he shoved his black hair back before reaching for his ring of keys. He was only too glad none witnessed his shaking hands. The car started before anybody noticed. His part, the hard part, was now over, he hoped. He had more confidence in the car than in himself right now.

He had sat on the side for two years watching, mainly their mistakes, and building something they'd talk about. He succeeded, though they razed him because they admired, that is to say envied his piece of work, and probably because they couldn't figure him coming up with the likes of a machine he had put together. His Dad had taught him to read blueprints at four am, before the man went to work and the boy to school, and after that everything seemed easy, except them.

He never minded a little jabbing, because it put him, and his car, in their conversation, if not their company, but tonight the two came together and made trouble for him. It got too much for him this time, them and their joking, so he spoke up, like he never had before, and the hard part was over now—he kept repeating that to himself.

He smiled at the worry in Dianio's face when Dianio started his car, because Sims knew weakness when he saw it, even his own, and Dianio's expression could not hide the fear of the older boy for the younger, so Joe pushed the accelerator down past idle, boasting, and Dianio looked away, pretending his gages in the floorboard needed supervision. Joe saw Dianio's worry in the older boy's face, and Joe Sims sat in his machine calmer for the moment.

Dianio threw his arm and index finger towards Rollins Road, a straight stretch of abused blacktop where they did their after midnight racing, except Joe Sims had only watched before. Tonight they'd be watching him, no, not he, his car, but he'd drive the car, so it was the same thing, however you looked at it. He'd be driving the car, and that took some special skill, because not just any joe could point and then maneuver a monster down roadway at full throttle and still manage control.

Sims left the eager crowd covering their ears when he scalded his tires for his audience.

Dianio waited until Sims finished before he left, and then the older boy drove off all law-abiding and civilized, with no rubber laid down now, unlike his usual stunts. Joe Sims watched Dianio's worried face in his rear view. Sims had nothing to do tonight; Dianio had that job Sims told himself.

Joe Sims could size up people about as well as he could cars, except he was afraid of people. Not really afraid though, just terribly shy. He didn't come by talking or conversation easily, but listening he did. Sometimes he wished he couldn't speak, but then he felt sinfully ashamed for such a thought, though he would have an explanation for his usual stifling shyness if it were so. He'd done all right at school because his mouth stayed shut and his ears open, except that worked better with his teachers than with his peers. He agonized with what made them like that. The car and now the boy stood ready.

James Dianio pulled up beside him, with the bully's gruffness back, and some of Sims's hesitation returned when he saw him. Probably James Dianio had ventured a talk with himself on the ride over, told himself that this little dweeb Sims had bargained for more than any parasite could ingest, and that it was his duty, Dianio's duty, to set this upstart mechanic straight before the twerp did real damage to Dianio's reputation.

Joe knew Dianio's plan because he had seen Dianio do it every time somebody bucked him, crossed him, because Dianio couldn't take a challenge, and he had to humiliate, make them back down right away before there was a showdown. Dianio would try the same thing with him now. Joe knew it.

Dianio strutted his old self again, hungry with an appetite that needed fresh feeding again because his ego was forever on the mend, but suddenly, and despite the flush of fresh worry, suddenly Joe didn't mind, didn't mind the perpetual smirk that Dianio had etched in his facial muscles, and Sims wondered why he had called out such a pitiful specimen.

He still had a lesson to teach, or a friend to make—he was not sure yet which, or that he had the strength for either.

Dianio did his usual intimidations at the starting line. Joe had seen it before, even knew how to do it himself. Dianio held the brake hard and then stomped the accelerator to send the car chassis lifting spasmodically upward toward the sky while quaking tires gripped the asphalt as the engine screamed to be let loose. Joe looked away, looked at his gages, as if they called for his attention, and he reminded himself again that he must let his old self go.

He'd have to think quickly now, for Dianio's ego was overdue for gratification and demanded revenge for the earlier humiliation. Joe Sims couldn't let this guy get away tonight. Dianio needed a lesson, instruction in how to be a human, for once. Sims couldn't feel much pity for Dianio just now.

"Tell you what I'll do!" Joe Sims screamed over the roaring motor of his competitor.

"I came out here to race punk!" the hungry Dianio taunted, letting Sims know that he had ordered their race, not the twerp.

"We'll race," Joe Sims shouted over Dianio's noise, and Dianio looked back at the flagger standing down in the ditch.

"You gonna race or not?" Dianio screamed back at Sims.

"We'll race," Sims answered, stalling for something to grab onto.

The flagger twitched his arm as he entered the fray of words between the two drivers.

"Start him in front of me," Sims shouted, as he tempted the other boy's ego. He had to get something done here, and he better get it right.

"Listen you twerp, I came here to blow you off this road!" Dianio's surging ego was in full throttle, and he'd soon demand his race. Sims must hurry and he knew it.

"I'll leave you sitting with me running backwards," Dianio boasted, and Joe Sims knew right then he had Dianio.

Dianio only managed forty miles an hour in reverse before the raging machine of Joe Sims caught him in no time at all and there was nowhere for Dianio or his car to go when Sims's machine started to crawl on top of him. Dianio saw the whites of Joe Sims's eyes as the spinning tires of the advancing car pushed Dianio's machine into the ditch.

The scalded ego of Dianio voiced little protest when the two cars finally skidded to a stop, and his head fell back on the seat. He turned the car off.

"Why'd you do that?" he whispered when Joe Sims walked over.

Sims looked at the defeated Dianio without starring, and Dianio looked to see what Joe Sims would do with his victory. Sims kept silent while he starred. Dianio started to move, at first a quiver, and then more, and finally he shook like winter had come, despite the hot August night. Joe Sims stood inside the door of Dianio's car, gazing at the picture of the Virgin and other stickers Dianio had on his car dash, stood next to him, and the crowd behind turned their curiosity away for now out of sympathy. Dianio would have preferred they drop dead right now and Sims with them, but he was not in charge anymore. Sims reached over for him.

The crowd of followers stepped back for the two to move, and Dianio propped himself up on the twerp's shoulder.

10

Lost Daughter

"I asked her many a time where she was. I'd call out and not just in the nighttime. I never gave any clothes away. Couldn't bear it. I knew I mustn't feel sorry for myself and go on like that forever because the good Lord told me there was work for me. That brought me back down a bit. I stayed on, kept doing what He had sent Jim and me here to do, though I wanted to claim every baby born in that building as mine after that," she said, pointing out the window and holding her pointing finger in the air.

Her listener smiled. "Blessed be the name of the Lord," she said. "I'll take you to your new place," she added.

"I knew after a while somebody had grabbed her. Nothing else made any sense. You know they had never seen a girl as pretty as her. Everybody had told me to hang on to her, and I had looked away just for a second. I guess that's all it took. I don't know how they got her that quickly," she said, her head moving from side to side while her pointing hand came to rest on the bed.

The attendant leaned across the bed sheets and picked up the frail hand.

"She was as pretty as you," the bedfast woman said to her new attendant.

"I told them just what time I saw her last. 9:19 am. I know, because I looked at my watch as soon as she disappeared. I don't know why. 'You never saw her after that?' they asked me. 'No,' I said." The woman managed to turn slowly onto her right side with a little help. "I never understood it, not for a long time. Nobody else could either. Course some thought I'd brought harm to my own daughter. People who knew me knew better. I suppose the authorities thought they must act, after they came up with no clues for her whereabouts. So they jailed me for about a month. Couldn't blame them, but it hurt then because I had too much time to think and I prayed too little.Imagined over and over how I might have prevented it." The woman's eyes fastened on the window again.

"The Lord takes away and the Lord gives," the attendant said, holding the elderly woman's hand and gently rubbing out some wrinkles from the tired face.

The restless woman stared at her attendant.

"I know. Of course I thought it myself—said it to myself many times—always hoping I'd get her back. People didn't know much what to say. Jim could hardly talk after it happened. I understood after a while, so I mostly talked to myself and to God. Jim and me, we would cry together though."

"You should rest now; I'll get you ready," the attendant said.

The woman felt weaker, and reached for her last cup of water in the room and grasped the comforting hand afterward before the elderly woman began to pull away.

"I had the ground, you know the dirt, and I had it scooped up where I saw her last. I had it brought to our back yard and grew flowers around it every summer. There wasn't any funeral, because there wasn't any body ever found. They asked Jim and me, seven years later, if we wanted to file a death certificate, but I declined. They said we might get some insurance money or something from our missionary agency. I never quit thinking that one day I'd find something. Maybe not her, just something, though I figured after a while she was gone. She was beautiful you know," she said, "as beautiful as you," she said again.

11

An Eye for an Eye

The words scrawled an hour earlier inside the apartment vanished as he ripped the notebook apart at the spine before hands trembling for help folded. They continued to shake.

He finished his supplications a half hour later, and he finally crawled out of his car carrying a photograph and fearing that she had lured him into her trap. Deafening requests to God had filled his car, for he dreaded the woman he would ask for pardon more than any man ever dreaded the judgment of God. He shook uncontrollably though standing almost upright and gripped by fears more gruesome than the hatred he once felt for his parents. His eyes shut for temporary respite from the outside of a dilapidated house warning ominously against the inside, as he envisioned her mind warped inside a room where eyes peered out, waiting for him.

Tree limbs overhung a dirt driveway and scratched peeling paint off the house and onto two cars sitting idly on flat tires, while carefree chickens huddled beneath the sinking metal heaps and inside a rotting fence disgracing the land it marked.

Nothing looked any better now than six months earlier, and he nearly collapsed shaking at the side of his car as horrific memories stalled his legs. Feet shoved his waffling body forward as he contemplated cowardice by retreat again. Sidewalk concrete pieces split by tree roots lay about, angled upward like decks of doomed ships, and he shot around the obstacles and past strutting proud fowls parading from beneath the dead cars. He acknowledged the feathered animals in passing with a whimper and then ignored them, struck with panic that her eyes stood working inside the house.

He swallowed another mental composition of sincere though pathetic remorse from the porch where he stood with his quivering legs. He would finally acknowledge all and everything—admit himself as the monster she knew—with no explanation nor excuse except confession. The paper was gone and his fabricated words too. The offender who had treated her savagely for four years now came to beg for mercy from his battered prey. One who had never extended mercy would now ask for it.

Rolled and peeling newspapers cluttered the concrete porch, while barking inside provoked a string of obscenities.

A kick to the noisy beast drew moans from the animal, and James Roan rotated his head from one shoulder to the other afterward for anything to lift his spirit. His eyes fastened on the hens again after the dog's whimpers stopped. The feathered fowls looked ready for battle, and he swallowed.

He was unable to remove himself at all from his car before—six months earlier—because the place looked horrific, a reality unimaginable if he had not seen it himself, but staring at him and indicting him. He had languished inside his car with unthinkable realization of what he had wrought on her. He had ruminated for three years over Jean Ramsey and finally acted after the unrelenting memories stopped his sleep altogether and his mentor ordered him to go.

He trembled as the door cracked open. The tinge of fouled air from inside the house found his nostrils and he prayed for death with resolve to flee were this prayer not answered, though his feet stumbled and then his tongue and he went to his knees on the concrete before he managed a name.

The voice sounded coarse and raspy in response, no longer young or even feminine.

The figure asked who he was again.

"James Roan." This time he included his last name. His trauma worsened when she asked how he came, for he feared this the beginning of her examination of him. Death he feared no more, for the past years had offered worse. His burden of himself and his past deeds he must acknowledge before the person wronged, for death would require it and would be delayed until done.

"We went to high school together," he said, but he meant to say the words differently, not as if he had planned a reunion. He had come to escape a doom that awaited him in life if he stayed away any longer.

Nothing she said he understood because her words sounded hard.

"I've come, to apologize." He caught a glimpse of her then, though unintended: Jean Ramsey after a quarter century. The house and yard looked better, and he prayed for real death now, as her face struck horror deep inside his soul and etched petrifying shock on his face, so his eyes turned away, regretful that he had seen her, and worse, that she had witnessed his shocked face. Her expression was one of sordid joy and haughty revelry that he had seen something of what he had done. She gave him no more words, though her silence of contempt and rancor contrasted sharply to her earlier youthful silence of innocence.

He had said she looked like a pig twenty so years earlier when he had first blocked her youthful step, with no thought that her future would sink and then disappear as his obsession with her would ruin her then and now him. He thought his cruelty fun then, though he knew later it was simply diversion, a compensation for his own lack. She did not retaliate then as she might have, and so he pitched the word at her again, and then relentlessly, and then for four years he robbed this girl of her future without pause or retaliation from her, and no one stopped him. She stood silently at that first examination, bearing his trial and abuse with the feeblest innocence, but today he would stand before her vehemence, a stranger whose face showed no fear nor respect for his desperation than he had of hers years earlier. The crowd witnessing the original spectacle between James Roan and Jean Ramsey had applauded his cruelty, and any affirmation at all for him, from anybody, nudged him forward then. Buoyed up by their support—they chorused his animal word for the girl—he continued his savage abuses of her until their graduation night ended it.

He now silently begged that Jean Ramsey would make some gesture behind the glass of a leaf-stained aluminum door: say anything to give him a chance, but after a minute of silence he would not endure another wait.

He had wasted, waited, three years already.

"I've got something in the car. For you." His mind forced the words out onto his lips.

She nodded after staring an intolerable span of time, as he finally got off his knees to make halting steps to the car.

The sterling platter was wrapped professionally and he lifted it from the car trunk before he froze with dread again. His fingers checked the card on the package before he sat it down and before his hand moved toward his face. He hoped she would not look, so he turned around, but he glimpsed her fearsome face before he grabbed his eyeball.

The flow of blood slowed after some time, so he resumed his errand, and gained more composure after he dropped the pain pills from his pocket into his mouth. He coaxed his feet and managed to wrench his body toward the house, despite the horrific physical appearance he must face again.

"I took a trip recently. And I bought this," he said, glimpsing her face with his remaining eye. He held the gift out for her, still gaping with pain as eternal seconds expired while she stared and before she called out Edgar's name.

"My mother is not feeling well," he explained. Roan expected more, and this hurt added to his swelling face. He stared at this offspring of the tormented, tall, unlike her, but sharing some of the face that she had had a quarter century earlier.

"Could I leave it?" Roan asked.

The son turned around.

"She said you can leave it," the messenger relayed.

The low tree limb prevented any movement of the door, and shoving the package through warped the strained aluminum frame. The host provided little help, and Roan disciplined his disappointment as he pushed his gift inside until the taker took it and then disappeared. Roan heard the dog again, but profanities worked this time without another kick.

"My mother says you may come in, if you can give her a few minutes," Edgar said, handing him a towel, as Roan humbled himself onto his knees again.

He had found a minister in his community when his anxiety over Jean Ramsey first started, three and a half years earlier. He had never met the man before he looked up churches in the yellow pages, though he told the stranger every detail about his worry and more than enough background at their first meeting. The minister listened without interruption and Roan returned a second time a week later before he asked what to do. The man told him, but James Roan fought himself for the next three years. After the abortive visit to Jean Ramsey's house, his prior three years of worry compounded and worsened to desperation and sleeplessness before exhaustion, so he visited the man again. He developed some health problems to multiply his emotional distress, and his doctor told him to avoid stress.

He had made a trip overseas after the abortive visit six months earlier—for some hopeful but failed attempt at forgetting his past—and spent a month sight-seeing without a camera, buying nothing but meals and a bed and the occasional train ticket. He took a roll of money along and used suitable and unsuitable occasions to hand small denominations of paper currency to people who looked needy. One recipient tried to rob him, but when Roan refused to accommodate the man with more money, the recipient-turned-robber produced a gun; Roan told the man to shoot him first and then to shoot himself. When nothing happened, Roan shouted that neither of them had anything to live for, but that he still had enough sense not to reward thieves with money.

Life fared better two decades earlier, because James Roan forgot Jean Ramsey after he went to study engineering at a distant university to get away from parents he hated. He settled into a routine that rewarded him four years later with a job that paid a good salary and provided him work that he liked. He socialized little, but married two years later after four dates, though this wife left within six months. She would try again with someone human, she said, as her last words to him. He went to a year of counseling afterward.

Six months after his divorce his parents died in a vacation accident, and while the inheritance negated any necessity to work, his boredom launched a contracting business that built houses. Business thrived while he worked without interruption and made shrewd decisions, and for fifteen years he managed to live unaffected by his past deed until he hired people who managed his company without him. He gave up on another marriage and he started to think about Jean then, but because he had moved away he never expected to see her and had no idea what he would say if he did.

She gaped at the face swollen from his missing eye, though her stare conveyed more curiosity than concern. He begged his memories to relent for once, to give him a chance, as his mind asked her stare to stop, if for a minute because he could not speak beneath such a gaze. Defiant silence issued from her instead, and his head dropped, like that of a beggar quitting before his humiliation becomes too much. She could have presented him with a sword he would have used on himself in any manner she wished, but he got on his knees again instead, though nothing happened, and he turned his face away from her and wished for death for the third time that day.

Her face spoke of her past tortures, alive with the ghastly history of herself he had inflicted on her. He wished he had brought a gun for her to use on him, but after she improvised another minute of silent torture for him she did push the door open, hitting the tree limb above before the bottom of the dilapidated door hit his knees.

His eye socket ran more blood after his stunned legs refused to move, and her face shackled his feet. She motioned him in anyway, but he jumped when the tortured pane of glass popped out of the aluminum frame and shattered fragments scattered across the concrete. He wanted desperately to run, but he pushed a handkerchief against his mouth and forced his body forward.

He worked to ignore the house stench. The smell produced a cough and the bloody handkerchief over the gaping eye socket came closer to his mouth. She pointed to a filthy couch while he pushed the handkerchief tighter against his flesh.

"This was my husband," she said, in a guttural voice, and she held out a photograph. "He died ten years ago," she added, her working eye forming all her expression, while her voice had an uneven scraping sound that gouged her words. The gentleness and beauty that he remembered but never noticed had clearly left long ago.

Roan gazed at the photo before his head drooped again while red moisture dripped.

"The boy who didn't pick me up," she said—though Roan knew—and he remembered enticing a boy to invite her to the prom. Roan's instructions had told him to not pick her up.

She had been elated that Joe Argyle, whom she hardly knew then, had asked her, and Roan remembered that she had a little gait in her walk then that he had never seen before. He cruelly stayed away to add to her false hope that new life was about to be, but when the night came she had collapsed in her parent's living room and missed three days of school. Roan and his friends teased her without mercy for her dream of some respite from her tortured life, but the boy he paid for the prank broke ranks and returned his wages, and for eleven days she had a friend—the only one Roan allowed her. Then

Roan threatened Argyle and her future husband stayed away until they graduated and both were free of James Roan.

He afflicted her with added torments after that, but not until the end did he plot a finale to celebrate his four years of torture that he saw soon ending. He had wondered if she would graduate, because her grades had deteriorated every year, but he made sure her name missed the graduation program. He instructed a student member of the program committee to scratch her name.

They might have been soul-mates. He yearned for one because he craved the company of another human. He knew that now. He should have tried warmth rather than cruelty, but he had remained stupidly callous to mask the severe loneliness she would see if she or anyone else came close. She could have been a friend for him, though she was beneath his family, and his surly parents certainly would have scoffed at a girl they never knew about and that he certainly never mentioned.

He was the needy one, but he never paid any real attention to her, never called her by her name. He had needed someone, and more, affection. He got neither from family. His parents, such as they were, remained too absorbed with themselves to notice him, or anything he might need, beyond physical things. They invented an excuse that an inadvertence caused them to miss his graduation night, but with them absent he craved something strong to numb his night. That was his explanation, such as it was: his excuse for extraordinary cruelty on one night she might otherwise have enjoyed, but for him. His parent's omission happened because they kept themselves for themselves, and paid scarcely any attention to him. After their fatal injuries on their last jaunt, their only child, then twenty-six, sold every asset of his parents, with no relic kept from his emaciated childhood, except their money.

On graduation night James Roan had watched as Jean Ramsey walked with tentative confidence up the stairs, but stalled and then froze, while waiting for a name that never came. For some seconds foot traffic behind her stopped too, but the boy behind soon stepped around the still figure when his name was announced and her name still unspoken and thus unclaimed. A teacher or administrator could have voiced her name, the name of the frozen human form on stage waiting yet for her name and her diploma, but Roan then let out a loud oinking noise instead and his classmates roared when she fled off the platform. He laughed hardest. Her family left carrying her minutes later, after he received his diploma and walked off the stage.

Her son Edgar moved over to the convulsing body on the floor. Roan now recognized Argyle in Edgar—something he had missed earlier at the door. Roan's single eye poured tears while his punishing mind absorbed another unbearable memory for all eternity. He wished he had made no effort at all: dying from lack of sleep and tortured by nightmares remained preferable to horror up close. He could have remained only miserable, but for his selfish effort to reclaim his sleep. He got up and staggered toward the door, covering his mouth to muffle screams that excited the dog. She motioned her son to tend the scruffy animal.

Six months earlier and after Roan's abortive visit to Jean Ramsey's house, he had found his pastor impatient when Roan suggested he could provide her with a house. Roan described her place in sordid detail to his listener, expecting affirmation and clerical blessing for his good intentions, but the pastor demurred. Roan was furious.

"I want to fix something!" Roan shouted, and their eyes met until Roan's eyes went to the floor, and then he charged out, angered that his generosity met with rebuff.

"I told you where you could start," the minister had shouted. The regurgitated words exploded in Roan's ears and he retraced his steps back into the study, where the man was waiting.

"I came to you for help!" Roan shouted.

"You'd better take something with you besides money," the pastor said, and the two starred at one another before the slim figure without warning plunged a fist into Roan's stomach. The bigger man slumped over.

"You bastard!" Roan said, bent over, as the bastard lunged at him again. The man of the cloth now pummeled his counselee without mercy—as much as a man well into his sixties could—until Roan finally pleaded for some relief, after his curses failed, but his assailant gave no heed to any such pleas.

Roan screamed, but the man still made no response, except to escalate his punches, and when Roan belatedly saw the man meant business, he started to defend himself. He presented no match for the agile pastor, who waited for further opportunity after Roan became completely exhausted, and then funneled blows so that Roan, overcome with more than just physical exhaustion, began to grieve uncontrollably. He now begged the man to stop, and with a final kick to the stomach, the man relented. Roan slumped in agony, and the pastor handed his phone to Roan and walked out of his own study.

Roan called his lawyer from his hospital bed the next day, but dropped his lawsuit one week later when he started building the new house.

When the landscaper had come to the nearly finished house, ready to put in shrubbery, Roan had provided a catered meal of pancakes and bacon and coffee. The foreman wanted to work as soon as the food was gone; he had not wanted to eat at all, but Roan produced some revised plans.

"I thought all of this had been decided," the foreman said.

"I was looking at some other options," Roan had said.

The foreman grimaced. With some prodding the landscaper acquiesced to some changes after disagreements between expert and homeowner provoked compromises. Workers sipped cold drinks Roan provided while the two argued over details. By the time of final compromises it was afternoon, and Roan had another meal catered to the house. The foreman was beside himself, and grabbed a shovel while the others ate.

Roan hesitated over anything like window treatments and managed to find that Jean Ramsey had one child, a son, and Roan contacted him. Edgar came back with answers to Roan's questions two days later with a phone call. Roan refrained from asking anything about the condition of the boy's mother, but Edgar did say his mother might be glad to see him, though she had mental problems and had lost her sight in one eye.

Jean Ramsey Argyle excused herself, and Roan asked his savage memories to relent so he might converse with Edgar in her absence, but her son fidgeted and hardly said anything before the door reopened minutes later. The boy had given him another towel for the seeping cavity where one eye had been a half hour earlier. Roan heard water running in another room and then he saw her nod at Edgar, and Roan felt uneasy after her son looked more nervous than he.

"You have a house for me?" she asked, taunting Roan with his secret. She smiled when her eye met the one he had left.

He must forgive the youngster for giving his secret away, though he thought they had an agreement. Roan glanced at him; Edgar looked away.

"Yes, yes I do," Roan stuttered. He could not get the picture out; his fingers shook, though no matter, for she would reach for the photograph.

"That's very pretty," she said. The photograph was upside down.

The night before had been frightful. He had prostrated himself from midnight to six a.m. to pray, and fell asleep afterward, frequented by horrific visions. He awoke screaming, and someone knocked on his door wanting to ask what was wrong, and he had managed to open the door and to give some satisfactory but scarcely truthful explanation to his inquirer. He called the pastor minutes later because he wanted final counsel before he went to see Jean Ramsey again. He showered before the pastor came, and managed to get some instant breakfast together after his guest arrived, but he could not eat.

The pastor held a hand that shook despite Roan's best efforts to calm himself. The man talked while Roan quivered, and when Roan tried to converse gaffing tremors erupted where his words should have been. Finally his guest placed an arm around the tortured man and found a sleeping pill for him before he put Roan into bed.

Roan told the man he had not slept in that bed or any bed for a month, and the apartment was so cluttered that the pastor wondered where any sleep was possible. Roan said the bed denied him sleep so he had stretched out on the floor: the discomfort helped him realize some pain needed a comfort greater than any sleep. It was something, he said, whereas for over twenty years he had felt nothing for his sin. He had told his housekeeper to quit coming a month before too, but he had hardly kept up the housework himself. Papers and blueprints lay strewn about.

The pastor held his hand until Roan fell asleep, and then the man prayed for another half hour at Roan's bedside. Roan never woke, though the pastor's voice was not soft, though his words were, and the man finally slipped away after his own exhaustion. He left his friend a brief note after he tidied up the man's apartment. At three o'clock in the afternoon he left, and Roan was still in bed.

Roan awoke two hours later.

Roan headed toward his car for a picture of landscaping around the new house, and for the first time that day, though almost never for the past three and a half years, he managed a smile.

She motioned Edgar to stay inside as she stood on the porch with her arms folded.

Roan forgot about the house after he spotted the glare in the garbage can. He started to gouge the other eye out, to be done with it, but his knees gave way as his hope started to recede. His mind reeled from his throbbing head, and he knew now he should have given both eyes for her, because without both she could hardly have wreaked vengeance he could see. He had left something for himself, and so she could still require more payment.

He dragged himself to the garbage can. She stepped back inside the house, and the two people behind the window watched as he fumbled through the trash before lifting his gift from the can. The bent and warped plate was ruined. He felt the dangling neck of a fowl protruded from one end of the mangled metal.

Roan pried the two sides of the expensive piece apart and pulled the warm animal close.

She rollicked behind the glass as he prayed yet again. Her son swiped his face, standing beside his mother while the dog went berserk. The animal's feet raked hard on the glass.

"Don't leave me like this," Roan screamed, and he ran feebly in the direction of the porch, not quite sure where he was going before he fell headlong in front of the gracious fowls crowded around the junk cars. Her rancorous laughter issued from behind the door.

He pulled himself up and groping about, crawled up the porch steps.

"What can I do Jean?" he pleaded from the steps. The door flew open.

The ferocious face lunged at him, and he heard Edgar's pleading behind her and then he began to pray for the first time for Edgar.

"You never even said my name!" Her hot saliva sprayed across the quivering body as Edgar's firm tug pulled and then drug her backwards. The door slammed and her curses erupted.

Twilight approached as he came to on the glass strewn porch. He would pray again, and he rested on the steps with hands folded, while the savage memories started to slip.

He found the mangled plate before he found and picked up the dead bird and he paused on the first piece of broken sidewalk with the animal under his arm. The fowls came closer to escort the blind man and he reached out to rub the majestic birds. The animals closed their protection around him before he started to stagger as he glimpsed the opening door above. Another's strength permitted his soul to walk upright as he started to fall—the mammoth mansions he saw up ahead—and he gave thanks for his counselor as he glimpsed the preparations for him, a monster now made clean and he started to weep uncontrollably. The dead bird dropped from his arm as his body fell.

Her body fell through the glass, as flesh ripped open and poured warm blood onto the littered porch before she tumbled to the ground below. The earth soaked up her pulsating blood, as the dog jumped through the jagged hole. Edgar tempted no more disaster, and he jerked the door open to get to a body dispensing his mother's last blood across unkempt yard. Her son shoved clothing against her flesh in desperation, as her head swung sideways.

The dog sniffed the cooling blood of a soul set free, as Edgar flung the animal by the ears through the air. The beast yelped, but found sure footing again and lunged at mourning chickens that stood fast. Each fowl protected ground around the body left behind, while the dog relented before the impregnable show of force. The animal retreated back to a master standing upright and screaming.

When she turned sixteen rumors circulated that she would quit school and end her misery. He found her and told her about his certain grief if she left, and she welled up with tears. She did stay in school, and he went back to congratulate her with a heartless sketch of her as a pig. He waited for her tears—they came in torrents—and then he offered a humiliating sympathy card. He asked for both back before she dropped them and afterward he stapled his grotesque art on the school bulletin board. The next day he instructed his followers to make an oinking sound every time they saw her.

12

False Witness

Waiting passengers gaped at the motionless body Stan cuddled on the bus floor, while one rapped on the glass incessantly until Stan swung around and screamed at her that another bus ran in a quarter hour. The woman struck the side of the bus harder and Stan swore at her this time after he lowered the trunk of the body to the floor and grabbed the radio. The other passengers caught their first glimpse of the deceased's face then. Some gasped while others ran up the street shouting.

The office received a piecemeal explanation, as the dispatcher managed to surmise the identity of the caller, the location of the incident, and that something awful had happened.

Stan wanted his memory of the past week vanquished and Joe and God forgotten, though Joe's crumpled body lay too close for imagination.

Joe had slammed face first onto the bus floor seven minutes earlier, dead instantly it looked to Stan, with Joe's obscenities dying in his throat on the way down to the pit. The final struggle with death recorded itself in eyes portending the catastrophe of the soul, for Stan saw in the horrific dead face that Joe knew his body abdicated before the man's body fell face first onto the floor.

Minutes earlier Joe had pointed to the brown building beside their 5th Street layover point and asked Stan about it.

"A church meets there," Stan had answered, his confidence bolstered with the opportunity in Joe's question. Stan's prayer of the past week and every sixty seconds for the past half hour for Divine aid had received answer. He reminded himself then that God prepared the future after an act of faith and Stan had reposed at last, grateful that God had finally blessed him with opportunity after hesitations and doubts had robbed Stan's confidence all week. Stan's eyes fixed on the church sign hanging crooked behind the door and he rubbed his hands together, pondering the inscrutable Providence that delayed confidence only to strengthen it.

Joe started to sneer and swear, and Stan panicked and had first looked away and then starred down the length of empty bus to stall and feign indifference at Joe's coarseness as more panic settled into Stan's soul. Stan had tried to pray again, as Joe escalated his crassness before a cough interrupted the man's perversity. Stan knew then he must spar with Joe—that he had known from the counsel of Sarah, Joe's wife—so he put his thoughts in order again and then prayed that God would rehabilitate his opportunity. Stan knew Joe needed God as much as anyone, like everyone, and Stan resumed his task then, but Joe paid no mind and brusquely interrupted Stan's effort with renewed vulgarity and then mocked without pause the storefront church.

"You owe God your life," Stan charged back, resisting the voice that told him to temper his words.

"My wife kept me in church a while, but I left. Smartest thing I ever did," Joe said and laughed. He looked intently at Stan, as if Stan had come to listen.

"No it wasn't!" Stan objected, but Joe smiled facetiously, while Stan despaired and then reciprocated the false smile of his adversary.

Joe laughed at him.

"I gave religion up long ago, and God sooner yet," Joe continued and Stan despaired and then without any more thought, decided to quit. In an instant he stood to go, to let Joe know he would not tolerate abuse of this kind, and satisfied too that God intended no conversation and certainly no conversion for this man. Joe motioned him to stay instead and Stan paused and finally dropped all resistance to the resistance, failing to object to anything else Joe said as the man raced over the follies of church, God, and religious nuts—like their own wives Sarah and Linda, Joe said. Stan stood politely and pathetically, stymied by Joe while the dying man used the last minute of his life to abuse his listener and his God.

"Blind leading the blindfolded," Joe taunted, and he had twisted around in his seat and toward the building, and made his last gesture of forty-six years with his left hand while he crafted words with perverse eloquence. He held the arm out too long and it never came back to his body until his right shoulder fell on it.

Paramedics lifted the body while Stan shoved on-lookers and gawkers back, except for the bothersome woman whom he permitted to stay in order to offer his insults to her, and then he insisted she have his seat on Sunday after he recognized her from his church. With her attention fixed, he turned his face toward heaven and spit. She told him she would pray, but he told her that he had already—some with other people—and she could see for herself what had happened and she should expect no better for her own petitions. She could still try, he said, with a facetious tone and smile, bullying the woman who showed more composure looking on the corpse than at him. He finally bid the weeping woman a mocking goodbye before he escaped into the rear of the ambulance with a paramedic who instructed him where to sit.

Stan dismissed the instructions the paramedic gave and the man reciprocated and ignored him until a call came that family would meet the body at the morgue.

The widow of scarcely one hour stood presiding over her shattered family in the parking lot, but the sight of the approaching vehicle presented too much for her too soon, and she collapsed and slid down the outside of the car door while Stan looked away, wishing for death.

In his shock he had forgotten the widow's name.

He heard her piercing wails from inside the ambulance, and his torment consolidated with unrelieved embarrassment when the driver slammed his brakes and Stan felt his own flushed body careening across a lukewarm corpse. The paramedic swore at the clumsy Stan as Stan slammed the padded wall rather than the paramedic, to retain what little composure he still had. Stan crawled back to his seat unhurt, desperate to go home to fatally injure himself and to tell his wife that she and the widow had ruined his life.

Two girls with long hair stood like soldiers beside Sarah—her name returned to him—and a boy physically smaller than the girls propped up his mother as the woman's knees bent. The paramedic unlatched thc ambulance doors and soon the family, enroute to see their deceased and practically carrying each other, shuffled toward the building. Stan watched from the window while he called his wife Linda from the paramedic's phone.

Linda bore significant responsibility for the whole catastrophe. She had found Joe repulsive after the two couples dined together at a restaurant a week earlier, but she had liked Joe's wife, and Linda defended her after Joe and Sarah had argued over Sarah's prayer at the meal. The next day the dead man's wife had called Stan, asking for help. He would never have consented, except for Linda.

The widow screamed when the sheet came back and her dead husband showed his face. The examiner asked for some information, but she moved away without answer, because the gaping open mouth looked too frightening to her, though the boy lingered after his mother turned her head. Stan winched, wished for death again, and that he had minded his own life. The girls contained any tears of their own; their brother kept his arm around his mother's waist. Stan stood unnoticed.

"I'm grateful he didn't die alone," she said thankfully, and Sarah tried to introduce her children to Stan, without success. The boy managed eye contact, and Stan peered back. Before Stan left the morgue, the boy's mother asked Stan to help carry her husband's coffin.

She called him at home. Her son needed answers and she could not address every question, not now. She felt remorse too for her earlier request, for involving Stan with Joe, and she needed to assure Stan that he had not aided her husband's death, only his life, such as it was. She had weighed her request of a week ago more times than the minutes Joe had been dead, and though she had some misgivings for approaching Stan, she had gotten nowhere with her husband alone and so she had. If anyone had responsibility for Joe's death, the blame lay with her, but Joe was gone now, and she had to manage the household of the living. She was asking for help with the young man in her house, who was asking about his Dad, asking questions that proved too much for her. If Stan could only help her a bit now, she could manage more of her responsibility later.

She had warned Stan for a week about Joe's anger and Joe's hatred of anything religious, and Stan hesitated until she told him more about the man she had tried to live with, while she had tried to live for God. Joe was a tough case, becoming unbearable for her, she said, so she was asking Stan for help.

“Thank you for coming,” Sarah said, as she sent her son back toward his two sisters and excused herself to Linda, but then she asked Linda to come and Sarah held her hand as the widow led them to the family room.

“I appreciate you coming,” she said again in the dark. She found the light switch and they saw her tears. A picture of the family of five on the wall starred at them.

“I was hoping you could say a few words at the funeral,” she asked, directing her words at Stan.

He tried to look her way while he starred elsewhere. Joe didn’t belong to him, wasn’t his care, his responsibility. She had told him so in as many words earlier. This woman could deal with this herself. Stan told himself that he had more than enough trauma: for her to ask for something more remained out of the question. A moment of courage opened his mouth.

“Sarah I really didn’t know Joe that well. In fact I barely knew him. I mean we worked together, but I really didn’t know him. When I went to talk to him . . . he was unresponsive.”

He stopped, but could not finish because his stomach objected violently as his heart left him and then accused him. Sarah nodded and the boy came into the room, and Stan hated her momentarily while he waited for the youngster’s hand, until he felt stung, and then he regretted and loathed his feebleness, his resentment, his shame. He knew he must forget Joe before he could do anything for the widow. He prayed that God would obliterate the man from his memory and then allow Stan to take his own life.

"Do you think my Dad will still drive a bus?" the boy asked, and Stan felt the hand of Linda.

Stan looked at the boy's mother, and sat down beside the lad on the green couch.

"Will he get to do up there what he did down here?" the boy asked.

"Maybe one of the girls could write down something for me, reminiscence or something. I could read that," he said to Sarah.

He shoved his words into a suit pocket after four unspoken lines on damp paper starred at him, and then he launched out with his own impromptu speech, pumped up by a sick heart that wrecked his elocution. He pleaded to his audience anyway, pointed to the casket with all ten fingers, and said everyone would go in one of these boxes someday. Joe did not manage fifty years, and some would feel their body leaving them before even that. Only our heartbeat separates us from . . .

Almost no one heard him, save the minister, who did not want to hear him, and who understood none of the words and he tartly asked Stan to find a pew before Stan had finished his speech. Stan hesitated but obliged and then stumbled off the podium before he tripped.

The minister spoke soothing words until the sobbing of the mourners vanished almost supernaturally. The oratory from the pulpit might have inspired or lead an army, as tears in the eyes of the bereaved fled from the silver tongue, while minds took comfort in assurance of the eternal bliss of the deceased.

Stan's head stayed buried. He grabbed a damp handkerchief from a coat pocket, while the handkerchiefs of other mourners went back to pockets, for the comforter in the pulpit had made the uneasy hearts of his listeners rest again.

Stan bolted from the floor, and then staggered in the direction of the coffin.

The minister winced and then motioned for Stan's capture by two seated in the second row, but the screams inside Stan's head told him to speak again. Stan fought the voice and almost silenced the roar inside his head until he recognized it; he started to take his seat again with the other pallbearers, but the deafening screams became intolerable, telling him to warn them of the awfulness of this separation, and that none of them wanted to be with the deceased. Tell them, the soul screamed at Stan.

Stan blurted everything he heard before the minister demanded his immediate removal with the minister's own screams.

Stan groped down the aisle now, scarcely a step ahead of his pursuers and tipping toward one side and then the other, like a drunk, and repeating the warning in a reverent rage. The minister barked to his designees to subdue the jelly-like and wobbling figure, while mourners sat in their pews mortified at the exhibition of such comedy at a funeral, and others at the pitched spiritual warfare between the combatants. Others sat resigned to pray for an end to the debacle, while the widow doubled over between her daughters, holding her face with a soaked handkerchief. The girls moved closer, but they had their own grief to manage, and each sobbed alone until one pulled her brother's head onto her lap and stroked the wet face.

The two appointed pursuers caught Stan behind the last row of mourners, and Stan dropped to his knees as the two men accomplished their task. Linda slipped out of her seat and the 5th Street church pastor joined the couple.

The coffin closed after the widow's request for a final goodbye. She leaned forward and kissed a dead cheek and stepped away as preparations for burial concluded. The box started to roll and silence engulfed the air except for the noise of the lifeless container moving from the church. It was hoisted off the rolling rack and laid into the back of the hearse.

Water spread over the grave and clouds sent more wetness over mourners who could not escape the drenching. No expectation of downpour sent defenseless bodies scurrying for cars and trees in the cemetery. Stan and Linda strolled toward a cedar until the tug on Stan's jacket stopped him, as the minister caught up to them.

"My Dad'll have to use the wipers on his bus today," the boy said, looking up at Stan.

"No, better than that my lad!" the minister said as he wedged closer to the boy. "There is no rain there, just as there are no tears. Your Dad is having a time he could never imagine in this life, and best of all, none of it will ever end!"

Stan's swelled face dripped with tears, but the rain made it hard for others to know, and he reached down for the boy, thanking God for mercy with words stronger than the nearby thunder, though softer than the stinging rain. The widow spoke her thanks to Stan, as Stan pulled the youngster near, while Linda took the minister aside.

13

Death in the Family

Nick pointed to the house and told his siblings dithering in the yard how much he hated her.

Married siblings came alone—no spouses dared venture near a mother-in-law who hated her own. Laura and John walked hastily from the tree and three sisters and four brothers looked for some sign from the twins as John held his sister's hand. He knew the prescience of Laura, but his siblings feared most anything from her, and two of them insisted on keeping their physical distance from their youngest sister because of her spirit.

She held one hand toward the sky, her arm moving like a diving rod.

The old woman looked at none of them as her nine children filed into her living room. Three of her offspring had not been in the house for twenty-five years. Her lawyer sat on his chair beside her, dutifully holding a lap of paper he shuffled, as her children stood—she asked none to sit. She pointed to markings on the floor.

"What's she doing?" Doris the elder sister whispered. Boyce stepped toward the door—feinting that he might leave—and Sally nudged her lawyer.

"Your mother has asked me to read her will." The man peered up as if to ask permission, but his client told him to read. Boyce sauntered back toward his siblings, his gait calculated to frustrate the mother he despised. She had places marked on the floor where each would stand, but Boyce stopped in front of the mark to spite her. Sally heard his voice and stared like a serpent poised to strike. Boyce wet his lips after he spat on her floor, a floor Laura had cleaned for her mother a day earlier.

Sally despised all her children, but Laura's twin more even than Laura; she loathed him. John had fled at fourteen in a convertible with the top down and without driver's license or car plate, and his mother never saw him until his father's death. The boy grew into a man of twenty-four years without a glimpse or word from her. She hated him for it, and all but two of her children despised her for her hatred of John and Laura. The family had been torn apart by hate from every direction.

John never asked for anything from his mother after he turned eight. He was too independent to tolerate the woman by his thirteenth birthday, but his father kept the boy from running off for a whole year before he did, but in his fifteenth year Sally discovered that the runaway had contact with her husband when she eavesdropped on a phone conversation and she confronted the boy's father on the back porch. James stalled at first before she threatened, and he admitted his secret standing up—because she demanded to know. The boy, he said, wanted nothing to do with the person responsible for his flight. She stood speechless for a moment before she struck the messenger on the face twice and the next day she threw her husband and Laura out the front door.

Every product of Sally's womb sided with their father and for the twins after the event, and Sally had kept every vestige of her family away for nineteen years because of it. She told them to stay away, and nearly everyone had avoided her for the decade after their father's funeral. Some broached her before—a remnant of her children tried to mend the shattered family—but when she recognized voices she laid the telephone down. Letters burned unopened.

When her father died, Laura got worse and she went to stay with her eldest sister after Laura started trekking to her mother's doorstep to ask for forgiveness and reprieve for an earlier courtroom drama and another part of the broken bones of the family that was unforgivable to her mother. The girl usually made the humbling trip with a small bouquet of flowers and always rubbing her teeth, a habit she started when her parents divorced. Her mother found amusement in the barefoot girl, prostrate on her porch and with a face smeared with ashes, but Sally had the police haul her away after she tired of the sight of the troubled girl. She told acquaintances that the writhing girl was more gratifying to her than the fun she had with her daughter in the courtroom a decade earlier, but only to a point, she added.

Ten years earlier she had told James she did not want him or John back, but she wanted Laura, she said, and she filed for custody of her daughter, senseless as claiming to want a child she had tossed out earlier with her father then seemed. She told her husband that Laura wasn't his, though he knew it untrue, but he might have lost his daughter anyway if the fifteen year old had not pleaded with hysterics that custody be with her father. The girl sobbed more than she spoke, recounting trials with her mother, while Sally scoffed from her seat in the courtroom.

When the youthful Laura finished, Sally told the judge that James could have her because nobody else wanted her. Family members surmised that Sally had only wanted to inflict hurt on the girl and had cruelly calculated that a mother's brutal rejection would prove too much for her daughter, and it did; the youngster wept bitterly and begged without response for forgiveness, and then she screamed for her mother. After that, no one believed that Sally had really wanted the girl back and that the trial had served the woman's insatiable appetite for cruelty. Laura went predictably worse after her mother turned on her, but Sally turned a deaf ear toward her daughter's future and the girl started having visions.

For the next nine years Sally had ignored a daughter institutionalized soon after by the elder sister who felt traumatized by her sibling's visions and behavior. Meanwhile,

Sally never saw her daughter once during the next nine years, but in February of the past year the aging woman had asked for Laura. Laura's doctors accommodated their patient's request to accommodate her mother, permitting Laura to spend a negotiated amount of days and time with Sally. The elated Laura welcomed this chance with her mother, but Sally was the same and regaled in abasing one who now habitually bowed in her mother's presence. Sally asked her once if she bowed at the institution, and Laura shook her head. Sally's acquaintances pitied the pathetic girl, treated like the fourteen year old she was twenty years earlier, but Sally's contempt for her never subsided, despite Laura's service to her. "Serves her right," Sally told astonished onlookers.

Sally tolerated Laura in her life again, because with rare exception Laura never confronted her mother, but more, Sally did need help in her old age, and she had no one else to ask, or that she would ask besides Laura. That aside, she had never forgiven Laura's court testimony twenty years earlier, nor the girl's stuttering tribute to her dad at his funeral, and she relentlessly mocked both in front of Laura.

Sally still blamed the family falling apart on John and after twenty years she had never forgiven him anymore than she had Laura. He had lost his wife in a freak car accident a year earlier and the wild behavior of his life that he had not curbed during her life, he stopped with her death.

He had a genuine religious conversion afterward, but his mother screamed at him when he told her, and then she erupted with a litany of profanity neighbors on the street still talked about.

Meanwhile, John had sat stunned and flabbergasted, expecting something different from a mother. He had hoped to reconcile that day with the cantankerous and cruel woman, despite the fact that she had spent an entire adult life doing nothing about herself and going from bad to worse. His long absence had blinded his memory of why he left.

After his wife's death and to be closer to Laura, John sold his business and moved back to the vicinity of his youth, with cautious but persistent hope of reconnecting with a mother estranged from him and her nine other children, but his mother did not find his union with God reason to have reunion with him, though he did ask forgiveness for his past and for his long absence from her life. She did not accept his apology nor forgive him, and she scoffed at any suggestion of divine mercy for one who had ripped her family from her, she said. When the impasse became apparent to him, he told her she needed God. She told him God let his wife die and waited. He paused before he spoke again. Afterward, she told him he had no right to put himself in the same sentence with the Almighty. He told her that the Almighty would stoop as low for her as He had for him.

Three months passed before he could visit again, and then she tried to postpone, for she was busy planning for a death in the family, her own, she told him.

The lawyer started to read, but he read too fast, Sally said, and she told him to slow down and read with deliberation and to start at the beginning again. He shifted in his chair and cleared his throat.

The normal preambles of a will were absent as the document went straight to naming new owners for her possessions. Missing were phrases about a soul returning to its Maker, conspicuously gone too any adjectives about "beloveds;" the will presented a list of mere names. Sally's eyes feasted on her children as her children heard any inheritance they might have had, doled out to people they never heard of, except for a cousin who would own the house they stood in. None had ever seen him.

The will specified that all her children would receive something, an equal inheritance—one dollar. "It's only a technicality, otherwise you'd get nothing," she explained, nine times for each of her offspring present. When the name of the eldest son came up—Reuben, who alone was absent—she said nothing.

Laura's home got the buffet.

"Thank you mother," the dutiful Laura responded.

"It's not for you. For the home. It won't be in your room. I gave instructions." Sally looked at children appalled again by her cruelty, as their faces gawked at her for some explanation of how even she could stoop to such level of depravity. Boyce bolted for the door behind the lawyer who grabbed his papers and now fled.

"Thought I owed you something?" the old woman asked Boyce, relishing his obvious consternation, but she did not wait for an answer. "Get out!" she shouted as her nostrils flared and her mouth opened wider and venom befitting her rage enveloped the room. The afflicted siblings knew the wrath of their mother, but they nevertheless dithered and shuffled, with few words amongst them before one turned to retreat and then all ran out onto the porch, except John.

"Let her be!" Boyce shouted back to his baby brother, as John tried to calm his mother.

She sat up at 6 a.m. thirteen days earlier with her plan ready to implement and she had stopped her mail with a phone call made from her bed still covered in papers from the night before. When a postal package arrived at seven anyway, because the carrier went out before her call came in, argument started with explanation that her day was full and the package must stay at the facility for another day.

"I'll call when you can come!" she shouted, and her arms wrestled the window until the wooden frame relinquished and screeched downward. Figurines fell from the sash and scattered across the living room.

"I don't come any ole time!" the man outside shouted.

"You go away, there's nothing here for you!" she shouted back, glaring at him behind the window, and sending profane gestures in his direction. She picked up pieces of angels while the verbal volley with her visitor turned more brutal, but after harangue between them wasted another minute too valuable to the driver, he yanked the package off her porch and stomped down the steps.

Most of her decisions followed quickly, but she had only started putting her affairs in order. When Laura had showed up at the doorstep Sally told her to come back the next day.

Some property would go to relatives and the buffet would go to Laura's home, but nothing more was designated for her children. She listed possessions and checked acquaintances' names before calling her lawyer to take down a will. Before he arrived she decided a nephew she knew through correspondence would have her house. Moreover, there were flowers and a dress to pick out and a yard and house to put in order, and visits to plan and preparations to make for her visitors. She scarcely took time for meals or anything else and she would let the phone ring unanswered for the day. She had placed pads of paper in every room of the house to aid memory after mental lapses sent her to rooms for a forgotten reason.

Laura had not left as her mother had ordered, but groped down the steps toward the small space she kept under the evergreen tree. She weeded and cultivated the gardens south of the house like they were her own, but that day she kept an eye on the house while she labored in patches of ground broken up for flowerbeds her mother had ordered weeks before. On three occasions she heard falls prefaced by profanities, but her mother moved about later, before the expected lawyer arrived. After finishing her work and with a bouquet of flowers placed under the tree, Laura reached inside her bag for her book and the water bottle she kept ready for such days. The nearby woods provided her the privacy she needed for a whole day outside, and she settled in to pray and read.

She had her forehead on the ground when the van from the home picked her up.

Boyce continued to swear at his mother, but he soon paused because now he knew why the old woman wanted them there: this sadistic pleasure she would miss from the grave, so she had devised one above ground. Her depraved nature must see their hurt and shock. That was all the pleasure she would have, but have it she would. If the woman had any faculties not destroyed by her cruelty, she knew she could expect no tears when she expired. Mourners they would not be—but sufferers they would be!

"There won't be any hell after you!" Boyce shouted louder, and his face reddened this time as his fists tightened.

"You took it all from me. Get out of my house before I kill all of you," she said.

"They'll shut the gates after you—and the world will be better for it. We will. You killed this family," he yelled, and then his head dropped. "You killed Pa too. He had his hell with you. You'll have yours alone!" he screamed.

Sally had contemplated and then decided on a flamboyant yellow dress. When Laura saw the picture the thirty-four year old was astonished and said so. Sally replied that she would not look different below ground than she had above and she severely rebuked the girl.

"I will look in death as I did in life," Sally countered, and Laura's face showed remorse for her remark, but not enough for her mother, so Laura walked to the fabric store in town for pattern books to finalize details on the dress, and after buying everything she sat at her mother's sewing machine to do what Laura had learned in the home. With her daughter working, Sally propped herself up in bed with her lists. She got up to try the fledgling dress on twice and after completion it hung ominously from the ceiling of her bedroom. “That will do,” she said to her daughter, and Sally sent her back to the flowerbeds.

Sally requested someone take her to the funeral home after the dress was done and when someone did—Laura did not drive—Sally wore the new garment. She led new acquaintances into the facility where they perused the coffin models on display, unsure of their purpose or Sally’s designs. Sally remained indifferent toward her troop of onlookers and the box that would hold her, while the women marveled over her easy acceptance of her looming mortality.

“James was buried in pine. It’ll work for me,” she said. No one except Laura knew who James was, nor did Laura answer to this group, though one asked who he was. Laura knew none of the group, and wondered how her mother had coerced them there. It bothered Laura too that her mother used her father’s name with pretense of affection, but Sally said nothing more too offensive, matching the yellow color of her dress with the available pine containers. After her selection she ambled about and had pictures made of herself in front of the coffin, because there would be no pictures of her later, she reminded those around her. “That would not be me,” she said. She had no doubt her future wishes would be respected, though none ever were.

She spent an hour in the funeral parlor before she conferred with the director and wrote him a check for his goods and services, taking care that Laura saw the transaction. He hesitated to thank Sally under the circumstances, but when she noticed his absent smile she scolded him.

“When my day comes, that funerary mystique will be absent or my payment will be rescinded from heaven,” she said without heaven's smile, and his expression changed. He nevertheless put her check in his coat pocket and Sally advised him on the intricacies of navigating through the doorways of her house and she produced a little map, which she gave to him, complete with dimensions of every doorway and room and then she shook his hand. She had insisted on the wake being in her home, but after her execution her body never came back to her house, and the house was torn down, after her nephew gave it back to his cousins.

Trouble developed getting out of the vehicle, so Laura knocked on doors her mother requested, and the visited came to the car to pass some time with Sally.

"I have already spoken to the florist," Sally explained. "You are to bring the flowers when she calls and she will arrange them and bring them to the house and then to the funeral home," she said. Laura was sent walking to the next house.

Laura came back to the car to report on conversation with her mother's mother and Laura offered to help the wobbling figure but Sally pushed her out of the way and slogged by her own devices toward the house where she came into the world. Laura fretted as her mother rang the doorbell and prayed when a woman who looked scarcely older than her visitor appeared.

Sally had not spoken with her mother since the woman had rebuked Sally at the graveside of Sally's husband and Alice Motley's son-in-law, a decade ago now, and from the car Laura could see the women squaring off at one another before Sally shouted for aid. The old woman had an impish smile and leaned on two bodies as they carried her back to the car, while Laura's grandmother, now back in the house, peered from a window. Laura managed a brief wave without her mother's notice.

Sally had talked to Laura's siblings over the phone and, Reuben, her eldest, swore at her. He had wanted her dead ten years ago. He mocked at her calling him, but she wanted her family with her once more, she said, feigning familial feeling her son knew she lacked. He scoffed and then laughed before he hung up.

She had pillaged through the folios and pictures of her family after she had the phone disconnected. One remaining photograph showed all twelve of them together, but she had not looked at pictures for nearly nineteen years. She had kept one wedding picture, but James she had scissored off. No pictures of John remained. She had destroyed them when he left, but she discovered one missed photograph of the twins together when they were six. John had his hand in front of Laura's face. That one she cut Laura off of and poked a hole in her brother's chest before she burned the picture.

John had gawked at the suspended dress the day before the lawyer was to read her will and she had crawled into bed for her visitor for tomorrow, not today, she told him with a snarl. She had tried to delay him, but he was insistent and irksome, wanting to see her then, though she was too busy. She had peeked over the top of her glasses and motioned for him to sit in the chair beside her.

"That's a nice dress," he said.

She hated his blather and her mind readied her speech for contention.

"My last dress."

"Mother you can't go yet," he said.

As if her business was his business, she thought.

"Laura bring your brother some lemonade," she ordered with her lips, as her mind readied itself for him.

John took two swallows and thanked Laura. His sister patted his shoulder, but Sally motioned to her that they needed privacy. Sally watched his body twisting from right to left and back again in search of a place for his glass.

"I make you that nervous?" she asked, still annoyed that he had upset her plans.

"No," he said, swallowing, and he sat his sweating glass on the wood floor. "I want to make my peace with you Mother—I've told you that." Her face reddened and she set about rebuking him, until he interrupted her.

"You aren't going to die Mother. God won't let you."

"Laura!" she shouted, "Show your brother to the door. He must be leaving now."

John's mouth had fallen open. He intended no hurt, but he could do little when his mother scorned every word.

"You can come again, tomorrow, when the rest are here," she said curtly to him.

He smiled belatedly to soften words that angered her, and he looked on her with pity, wishing he could undo all the hurt he had caused. The old woman needed a fresh work of God in her soul, and maybe one that her soul had never glimpsed. She pulled her body further up in bed until the top of her head was higher than his. John forced his separated lips together and managed to stay seated until his sister came. He walked behind his escort to the door.

"She's not going anywhere, yet," he said to Laura. Laura rubbed her teeth.

If they had experienced a normal childhood they might be less close by now, but the twins kept together as they lived apart. They wrote letters, coupled with trips from the father and daughter to visit the runaway. Together they had tried to persuade him to come back and live with them after the divorce, but he would have none of it. That would be too close to his mother, he said.

Laura was in therapy before her sixteenth birthday, but her problems escalated tremendously with the death of her only real parent. Her sister was no help. James had left his paltry estate to Laura, blessed by her siblings, and coupled with gifts from John and some others, she was moved to an institution where John continued to visit, but he stopped after his wife died in the accident. When Laura's letters to him remained unanswered, the frantic woman ran off by means unknown and managed to take a bus to the next state, where she found him near total collapse with grief. She brought her father's Bible, intending it as a gift for her brother, but he was scarcely aware she was there, so she read the book aloud.

She read for three days, from morning until they retired, her slow speech fractured though usually coherent. Her listener improved by the third day, and she started to put the book down, but he pushed it back into her hands. He listened as attentively as any school boy to his sister and finally after almost a week he took the book from her, and they talked late into the evening.

She left after another week and he went back to work, but ruminating over all his sister revealed and after two months he drove to get her for his baptism and told her what God did. His mother was not impressed and fearing for Laura because of it, John cautioned his sister about telling their mother anything about her part in what had happened. "He should be concerned about how he wronged his mother rather than his God," she told Laura.

"You know they hate her?" he had said to Laura, as they had walked in the garden the previous day and after their mother threw John out of the house. Laura reached her arm around her brother and rubbed her teeth with the other hand.

"But they're coming—except Ruben. He said she should be in hell by now—thought I was calling to say she was dead. He wouldn't say anything else to me, seemed upset I had called," John said.

Laura fidgeted with her teeth, as her eyes rolled back.

"Ruben, I know. He didn't want me back here last year, he told me that, but he didn't mean all that stuff he said about her. He couldn't kill anybody."

Laura had continued to hold his hand, and they walked under the tree where she camped when the old woman ordered her out of the house. They prayed for their sisters, Sue, Jane, and Doris, and then Reuben, Alvin, Nick, Christopher, and Boyce—and their mother. Laura swung one arm wildly into the air while she petitioned God.

Older siblings were gone when John ran off, but because they took their brother's side, and then their father's side, Sally lumped all of them together. She remained just as hateful after her desecration of their father's grave, and after that those who tried to salvage any relationship with her quit, except for Laura and John.

She had attended the funeral, though she refused to sit with her family, but when James's casket was lowered into the ground, she stalked toward the hole in the ground and in front of her children spat on her husband's coffin three times. Her own mother slapped her, but Reuben had grabbed her, vowed to kill her, so Sally pressed legal charges against him. He was ordered to stay away from his mother.

"To be rid of you will be my reward!" the old woman shouted now to John, and she might have plunged down the steps in her haste to get at him, except Laura caught her mother's tottering body as a cane thudded hard against his back. He fled backwards into the house. The old woman jerked away from Laura and shoved herself through the doorway, and John saw Laura cross herself as Sally's arm raised.

Strained voices came from the room, but none understood save Laura and none moved until the shot.

The old woman fell into her chair, as she finally rested in the comfort of the pillows where she had first planned her vengeance. The gun lay on the floor beside her, but her children paid her no mind and her body slumped forward when she saw them hovering over him. Her head plunged down into her lap.

The body on the floor lay still and Laura touched it, but the warm flesh did nothing. His brothers wept, as Doris ran outside to call the police. The old woman picked her head up and sat back in her chair. Laura pushed at the robust arms and caressed the motionless face of her brother with her own wet flesh. She began to sob and Sue and Nick pried her off her twin.

The examiner pronounced John dead and found his own way out of the house. He detoured around the buffet at the sidewalk edge, hauled out of the house by Boyce and doused with kerosene.

"You can live with me," Boyce shouted to his sister-- on her knees under the tree—as he tossed his match.

A police investigator arrived with the rejected package of days earlier now inside a plastic bag, and Laura saw Reuben cuffed in the back seat of a vehicle parked beside another that held their mother. The oozing package at the post office had been turned over to the police, who had traced a feeble attempt to poison Sally to Reuben. Any other day Laura would have greeted her brother, but first she must pray for her mother.

Three years later Sally Hatchings paid for the murder of her son with her life, but three months before her execution she asked Laura to speak at her funeral.

The next day Boyce threw his sister out of his house.

14

The Accountant

John Savoring milked cows for fifty-six years before a cow kicked him in the forehead, and his body fell face down in the browned bedding as his muffled words died unheard in filth. His wife shot the guilty cow three times. To the cow the shooter extended none of the mercies usually extended to animals in long company with their human keepers. In tears of fright and anger the armed female remembered her plan and stumbled back to the house.

"Your Papa's done milking," the hopeful widow whispered to herself, fashioning words carefully as her lips quivered until anger returned and overtook any trepidation she had over taking a life. She shoved her less than agile feet over the threshold and into the house, as a strong eye surveyed the upstairs without turning her head. She pushed on through her kitchen to put the rifle in the corner and for a brief second contemplated it before she rummaged instead through the kitchen drawer for her knife.

"He wanted the best for you," she continued.

The woman's words, none too soft, found their way to his alerted ears.

He stood on the landing outside his room.

"Your Papa only wanted the best for you," she shouted again when she spotted him. She instantly regretted her tone. It sounded all wrong.

"He wanted milking to go on," he said.

Her anger returned and burned at his retort.

"Something wrong with that?" she asked, looking up again, and now regretting another poor choice of words. Why she had drawn him into an unnecessary verbal spar, she did not know, except that she loathed him.

"No mother, nothing wrong with it. He say anything before he went?"

"Hollered one time," she said, as she instantly realized she had made up the answer in her haste. Never mind that, she reasoned. Lying presented her with negligible worry right now. What mattered was putting an end to the Savoring name and her misery because of them.

She started up the stairs. He started down for her, out of respect, but she waved him back. She must avoid any suspicion.

"I heard him, came running, but he was dead," she offered. "The cow did it gawked at me. She was proud of her feat—oh she did gall me with that look. I came back to the house then, couldn't help it, but I couldn't stomach the hussy—sorry if I disturbed you with the shooting."

The pretense of any concern for her son was hollow to him.

She paused on a middle step and pointed to the rifle standing in the kitchen corner.

"Don't want that cow's flesh on my table. Guess I'll call Chandlers," she said, now finally reaching the top of the stairs, and nearly out of breath.

"Chandlers?" he asked.

"The rendering people. Don't want her on nobody else's table either. They'll grind her for something."

"You want me to call the funeral home?" he asked.

"No, I'll call," she said, as her body movement revealed the print of the kitchen knife in her back pocket. "Yea, Curtis, I guess. They've put many a Savoring in the ground though your Papa never cared much for them. He kept back part of their payment when they dropped your Grandpa's casket into the grave. John said the old man must have rolled over on his side on account of that bounce." She wiped her face.

"You want to see your father before they take him away?" The two sets of eyes met close up for the first time that morning.

"Sure. Give me a few minutes and I'll call Curtis," he said.

He called the police.

She stepped into their bedroom to rest her feet and her eyes settled onto the messy bureau she always complained about and tried to get her husband to clean up when he was alive. He kept everything there, everywhere, in and out of drawers and on the floor too.

The farm was his life, and he had been a decent provider when he could provide. When milk prices started to slip and feed prices escalate, he couldn't keep up, and so he worked harder, but that didn't do enough. His was a Savoring response to any problem, no matter if more work worked as a solution or not. He had to know, but he was too old to do anything else, and they owned all those cows and machinery and buildings and land. It all must be worked because they had it to work, she reasoned that he reasoned.

He never cried on her shoulder, though. He was too proud. Fitting he die working because he had lived to work for the farm though certainly not for her. He never spoke of death, because she figured he figured his demise would bring the end of the farm. That was the Savoring; his own death only mattered for what it meant for the farm.

She suddenly remembered that she had kissed him at the breakfast table that morning, as she sometimes did, out of habit, and not from any affection. "You make too much fuss over me," he had said, but he did smile when he said it. She frowned now, remembering that she would've known the kind of man she got if she had known better the Savoring family when he courted her. The whole bunch did nothing but work and John worked her. John Jr. was different, and his father couldn't figure him but his mother could. She resented him, hated him, even more than the family name they all bore.

"Ready?"

His voice startled her, but she had remained on the bed till he came, moving her thumb in and out of her fist. He sat his suitcase beside her, adding instant insult to her knowledge that he had only stayed this long for his father.

"I guess you were just waitin'?" she asked, turning to him and resisting the urge to say more, to tell him the truth about himself and how his selfishness ruined the place he now stood ready to abandon and her with it.

He nodded.

"I figured as much," she said, with disgust in her stomach, though disguised in her breath.

"His calculations were all off," her son said.

"I figured that," she said, with a modest but deceitful smile, and confident again and shaking her head at the bureau for a bit of show. "Send me a bill for what you covered. I know it's no small amount. I'll pay you off when I sell." She almost laughed because he would have no use for money afterward.

He had stayed on the farm. It didn't help being the only boy in a family of six kids, nor the youngest. When his father looked for someone to continue the Savoring farm he naturally looked to his son. The boy was never good around mechanical things or dust, but he liked to count, and his father put him to figuring feed formulas and rations, and by the time he was a teenager, his father gave the fourteen year old the farm books to keep. The youngster always put on a shirt and tie in the house when he did the books. The boy loved figures more than the farm, and his father knew it as much as he regretted it.

"Gotta do more than be able to count your profits—have to make them too," his father had said, but the boy had no interest in the farm itself. He did well in school though, and soon his teachers were saying he should do something with math. The boy knew it before the teachers told him, though the father saw it before either one, but bearing down on the boy to farm didn't work, and by sixteen the relationship between the two became quietly distant after it had become heated.

John Jr. continued to manage the books for the farm, but got another job in town, paid his parents some rent money though still in high school, and lived almost as a stranger in the house.

After a while, the man was just glad the boy didn't run off and his father returned the boy's rent money, despite his wife, who eventually relented under pressure from her husband first and later her psychiatrist. When John Jr. went to college, his father nearly had a breakdown, but he did manage to visit his son once at the college. The boy was not so far away he could not help his dad manage the farm books, and so the old man still had some hope. To his silent delight his son took a job at a local firm when he graduated, and the boy came back home to live. The old man gave up on expecting his son to find any interest in the farm by then, but he did like having him in the house, though neither saw much of the other, except occasionally in the evenings.

Eighteen months earlier John Jr. told his mother the farm was losing money hand over fist. She told him that the old man didn't have much left in him, and maybe they could keep it afloat a while longer, if it didn't get too bad.

She had asked her son for the past months how bad it was, usually every month, but he told her not to worry and she fumed after she realized she would inherit the debt her son would pass off to her from the deficiencies of the Savoring she had married. The younger Savoring bought the groceries and other essentials that his father thought his farming was buying, and he handed her the bill for that too, minus his third.

He held her hand, figuring he could avert her move if he had a hand on her. The two of them walked slowly toward the barn without speaking until the sound of the distant police siren came within earshot. He heard it first, and felt her rough hand ever so slightly start to pull away from his grasp. She knew now he had not called the ambulance and that she must move rapidly. He gripped harder as she tried to break his grip, but she managed to pull free of a hand that scarcely had half the strength of her own. His hands had only ever maneuvered writing instruments and calculating machines and registers. Her hands had massaged and pulled on stubborn cow teats, hoisted wrenching hay bales over racks taller than she, and planted fence posts in ground too rocky for good pasture to grow.

She stabbed him in the stomach before he knocked the knife away with his suitcase. The commotion roused a moaning old man out of the straw, but today he would not go back to work.

15

Controverted

The youngster had turned twelve, but the boy quit celebrating when he got born again and told his grandfather the first birth had no meaning and made no matter after the second. His grandfather vaulted into a fit of unmanaged anger and retorted that it was better to not have been born at all, if you's born again. The whole commotion stung the boy too, but less than it did the old man for the weathered farmer had hoped to keep the boy a heathen like himself. Not only were his hopes dashed, but now he could hardly stand to look at his grandson. The boy was made new, the youth said, though his grandfather suffered terribly over the whole thing. His grandfather might have given up and turned the boy out if he had not promised his daughter he would raise the youngster after the old man could see nobody—his daughter and the boy's father included—really wanted the bother of the boy. But the boy was no real bother to him, until the boy got religion.

The boy had never gone to church, because of worldly and selfish parents whose Saturday nights went well into Sunday mornings and then because his adoptive grandparent fumed at anything remotely religious. The old man kept the boy at home on Sundays and at some distance from any house of worship. After schoolmates started talking about their rambunctious Sundays and of everything imaginable, from dinners on the grounds to healings of the infirm, the boy began his questions. He asked his grandfather if he could attend an evening revival service. John Surly put his foot down right away, said absolutely not, but the youngster ran out before dark against explicit instructions to stay put that night and afterward came back saved and the old man wailed, until his anger sent him into the woodshed to fetch his straps.

The boy proclaimed the evening in detail to the man after the event: visions, healings, tongues, exorcisms, handstands, holy somersaults and all. And while his grandfather lashed him the boy warned him in the loudest adolescent voice in the surrounding hills that the devil was thanking the old man for his service to the kingdom of evil. The youngster's tears from the thrashing conveyed no remorse, only the boy's temporary pain, and thus provided no satisfaction for the old man that the punishment would stop the behavior, for the boy screamed his thanks to his tormentor and to God for the honor and blessing of persecution coming so soon in his new birth, he said. The man finally threw his whip down and stomped into the woods in profane disgust, swearing louder with every step he put between the boy and himself. The boy hardly heard a word of the profanity spewing from the old man while the youngster sang his thanksgiving to God in such a loud voice that his grandfather stomped a half mile to get away from all the noise and then he spent the night in the woods alone. If the man had acquiesced in prayer, he would have prostrated himself before God as a most needful supplicant. As it was, he buried his face in the forest floor of leaves and twigs and wept that half of the night not given to continuing profanity for having forgotten a bottle that could have relieved some of his new sorrow.

The boy had called him words during the thrashing that the old man didn't entirely comprehend, and he didn't have a dictionary, nor could he read, so he would eventually make a trip into town for inquiry among the scrupulously educated staff at the library.

Charged with the boy's upbringing, the old man had tried to steer the boy in the right direction, which was for John Surly to provide strong direction away from the wrong direction. He had hoped the youngster would get an education of common sense and decency before the boy lost any sense he had with prior to this religion, but that didn't happen after the new birth. Surly knew it for sure days later when the boy told John Surly again that the old man was a reprobate and a heathen. The boy's grandfather didn't precisely understand the meaning of his grandson's big words this time either. He nevertheless figured they meant something disrespectful to him, and that such words were thus the first fruits of the boy's new lunacy. He had told the boy in the beginning that church pandered to nobodies and gave hypocrites excuse for their sins, but he would let the boy make up his own mind. He didn't actually mean the last part, but he wanted to show the youngster that he wasn't going to force anything on him. He failed though, because John Surly could not keep his grandson Ben from falling into the abyss of the things of God. Now he would try to get him out.

Surly's wrinkled face had looked excessively sober after one of the library staff read the definitions. Startled though he was to hear the meaning of the words, the boy's antics that pain-filled night made more sense to him now, and he resolved then and there to fight harder to wrestle the boy from his youthful weakness for God. He thanked the staff member quietly, but before he turned to walk back to his truck and because he appeared visibly shaken to her, she said some educated people despised religion too, and he felt better then. When the library worker reassured him that he wasn't alone in his opposition to religion, that in fact she herself was opposed to it, the old man had starred back at her, blank in expression, until she smiled. After that he told her something about the doings of his grandson, and he felt better for a while because the woman offered her support and told him too how she had handled the issue with her own children, quite successfully, she had said, and she smiled again.

The man endured six years of the boy's religion before any change came. His interventions failed to purge the boy of religion and nearly eclipsed the work of the farm, at least for a while. Then Surly began putting more work into the farm again for an education for the youngster, after his own efforts to bring the boy back from God only seemed to bring the youngster closer.

Surly would see to it that the boy would go to college whether he wanted to or not because Surly surmised the boy smart enough, and so he began to consider his savings insufficient for the venture, and began to add to them as he could. The boy needed higher education, because maybe they could do with the boy what he had failed to accomplish. Beyond that plan, the old man had no other. If he had believed there was divine aid to aid disbelief, he would have prayed for it.

John Surly possessed more pride than most, but his zeal against religion was greater. So he asked for private tutoring at the library, though his grandson Ben got word of the acquired literacy, and gave his grandfather a Bible one Christmas. The boy had of course wanted to give that gift for some time before he did, but the boy had feared the reaction of a man who habitually swore in the presence of things holy. The old man had never allowed a holy book in the house and he did grimace at first, though he took it anyway and then managed with difficulty to thank the boy without expression. When their Christmas dinner meal was over, and he was out of his grandson's sight, he slipped the Bible under his mattress, intending it to stay there until John Surly was dead or the house burned down. A book never opened was the same as a book never owned, he said to himself.

On suitable occasion, and early on, he had confronted the boy with some of the arguments the library staff member provided during his tutorials. The old man sometimes rehearsed the arguments until the late hours in preparation for any opportunity with the boy, but the boy's religion was so abysmally void of thought that anything the old man said the boy summarily dismissed as coming from a reprobate and heathen and thus of no consequence. The old man usually erupted over this demeaning of his new learning, and more often than not, he went to his bedroom after such exchanges to drink, but he never went to the woods again, no matter how upsetting the nonsense with which the boy defended nonsense. His tutor had cautioned Surly that he must avoid all appearance of being bested in argument with the boy, even when he was.

Soon after that, the old man renewed his energies for making more needed money for college for the grandson. The still that was in the woods, that he had stopped working when the boy came to live with him, he put back into operation.

The old man's final despair began after he took the boy to college, for John Surly would now sit alone in his house once again, as he had for ten years before he took custody of the boy. Despite their troubles, the old man had generous affection for the youngster, and after he had said his goodbyes to his grandson in the parking lot of a dormitory—and to a substantial cashier's bank check handed to the eighteen year old—he drove two blocks away and had himself a good cry and a drink of whiskey. The drink could not stop the grief, however, and the good sense of the old man committed him to a cheap motel on the edge of town until he crawled out of the motel bed the next morning with the drinking done but the grief still intact. He got home by afternoon and sat idly on his front porch the rest of the day. He once considered getting the Bible out until he thought better of such thoughts, and reminded himself that in weakness there is no strength.

When he did not come to the library for his weekly tutorial that week nor the next week, he received a letter from his tutor inquiring as to his absence and he went for the next session. Little of their usual topical subject was taken up however, as his tutor listened to the old man's reminisce of the boy's better years with his grandfather.

It would be the last time the tutor saw the old man. When he wrote her in his own hand a hefty letter a month later and told her the reason for his absences—but that he did want to see her again in time—she returned his letter with her own, telling him not to come back.

Ben Surly walked up on his grandfather's porch some weeks after, with his first semester of college nearing close, and he embraced the old man before he saw the Bible he had given.

"Reading that?" he said to his grandfather. The old man had the Bible in his lap.

"Not just reading," he said, "living. It's meant for living people, who wanna go on living, even after we's dead."

The boy reeled in shock, and turned as he stood ready to leave for a moment, and Surly surmised now that something for sure had happened to the boy. The old man had written the youngster a letter with some detail of his new life, but he had not heard from his grandson after that and worried. He was right to wonder because the boy loved the man who had cared for him after both parents expressed the wish for the boy to go elsewhere. The boy never took the old man for granted and had tolerated his grandfather's quirks because of it. This latest quirk might be intolerable to the boy.

"I couldn't answer those letters," he said, and the boy for the first time dropped his head, not in shame, but regret.

"I should never have given you that," the boy said, intending no disrespect for his grandfather, he continued, but for the book, because, he said, that book was another matter. He tried to wrestle his gift out of the man's lap, to his grandfather's amazement, but thc old man's farm hands were too strong for the youngster's weaker fingers. The old man looked up at an expression he hardly recognized as from the boy.

Ben had just extricated himself from the book and its superstitions he said. It took scarcely one substantial conversation to cancel a conversion seven years in the running. He had tangled with a philosophy professor of his and came away days later convinced that he couldn't be convinced of anything anymore, least of all something so mysterious and beyond reason as a talking god, like you find in that Bible, he said to the old man.

"Philosophers call those matters metaphysical, and we know now we don't know anything about them," the boy said, punctuating this newly acquired learning with a youthful vigor that indicated there were more reasons to come.

His grandfather listened to the whole explanation, because the boy had a large liturgy of justifications of why he had correctly given up what he had in ignorance gained years earlier.

"I should have reasoned it out long time ago—or listened to you—" Ben said, while shaking his head and staring in amazement at the old man resting his head on the chair back. He told the man about all the horrors of religion, about the Inquisition, the Crusades, Henry the Emperor being humiliated barefoot in the snow for three days by the Pope, the unloading of whole peoples from one country to another for not being Christian, Yankee Christian fighting Rebel Christian in the Civil War, and the World Wars, the rack as punishment for heresy, the index as the prohibition against thinking, the treatment of Galileo because of math and his telescope, the fear of Descartes for his writings, and the preacher in the next town who warned all of his parishioners about attending those god-forsaken colleges.

"How did this happen?" the boy asked after dinner, and the old man reclined.

He said that someone or something had laid the book on the old man's bed one night, though now he knew it was the Holy Ghost. The boy objected and asked how he knew that, but the old man went on without answer. He did say he still didn't know how He got in, the doors stood locked, he was sure of it. But he woke up and felt the weight of the book on his chest and opened. He had sat up, looked around, couldn't see anyone. Light came in and illuminated a sentence—a verse—so he read it. He had no trouble reading the words, but when he did the house whistled and the doors flew open, as a gust of wind plowed through. He thought a storm had hit until he looked outside from his bed and saw nothing at all stirring in the dark outside. His bed started to shake, and he fell out of it when the Word of God struck hard in his crusty heart. The boy objected again, about the wind this time, but the old man would not relent before the protests of the youngster.

The grandfather had told the boy more than he wanted to hear, and Ben burned with remorse for the old man and anger at himself. He disdained his part in this delusion.

"I thanked Him for you, boy. Told Him I stood justly damned myself, and I got on my knees right then before the Arbitrator of my doom, but He told me He came to save them that was lost."

The old man sat back down in his chair then. His grandson could not endure the look of the old man, the happiness on his face, because the boy knew the source and that it had deluded him once. The old man had possessed a bitter face, one worn with the years of scorn and hate. This face was new.

16

Dinner

Nobody came to Claudia's party on Friday night so Claudia invited her own friends after eight thirty. She asked her mother if the older woman could give her and her guests some privacy.

"Sure, Honey. I'll just be in the outer room if anybody needs anything." Claudia's mother showed her affection for her thirty year old daughter openly with a kiss to the cheek, while Claudia's friends taunted their hostess before her mother disappeared. Claudia stiffened . . .

"I love her," she said to her friends, "You're not here to mock me; I asked you here for some fun."

Claudia's friends continued to revile Claudia, though after a while the group decided to behave the rest of the evening lest they not get another invitation out.

Claudia had made them for play, but they interrogated the girl when they could. Claudia enjoyed the girls at times, as ephemeral as they were, for they represented the extent of any friends her own age she wanted. Claudia was odd to outsiders, though not morose or unpleasant, so she was ignored by others, and her mother served as her protector when needed and sometimes when not. When she protected too much, simply for the desire for adventure, Claudia let her friends emerge, though they presented themselves as teasers more often than friends.

"Mother—could you come?" Claudia asked.

"Yes," her mother said, as she pushed her head into the door.

"My guests must be going now. They have disgraced themselves and must do penitence."

"Confession too?" her mother asked.

"Both I'm afraid Mother. They insulted you—to me."

Cynthia Ambers knew Claudia's guests too well, and she scolded the visitors while shoving them toward the door.

"Now, that's done," her mother remarked, returning from the door and slapping her hands together. Claudia had seen the whole thing.

"Mother?"

"Yes Claudia."

"They're not very good friends are they?"

"No, I'm afraid not."

"And they weren't very nice, I mean to you!"

"Nor to you Claudia."

"Then I should say, good riddance. And mother, oh mother, I saw you kick them in the seat of their sit downs, I mean for me!"

Cynthia Ambers laughed.

"Mother the intruders are gone for now."

"I'm glad Claudia," the woman said.

"Mother, I invited them."

"I know Claudia."

"Why did you tolerate them Mother?"

"You needed to have a party Claudia."

"I invited the wrong people," Claudia said, before she paused. "Mother, did I invite you to my party?"

"Well, I didn't get an invitation. Not that I recall I mean."

"I'm inviting you now mother. We shall go into town, and I will buy you ice cream after I take you for some dinner."

"As you wish Claudia. Shall we go?"

Claudia held out her hand for the woman she loved.

17

Once Upon a Time

The frenzy showed no sign of abatement until the moderator scrambled toward the audience with hands waving.

"Thank you," he said, minutes later, the crowd finally hushing their chants after they grew tired of his pleading. "In fairness to our other debater we must give him equal opportunity to respond. Therefore, I ask you to refrain from any more interruptions while he speaks."

The moderator thanked the audience again and William thanked the moderator. William headed to the seat of his manager Norman. The crowd started to point at them and some laughed.

"I request that the candidate return to his podium," the moderator said to William with some firmness, though for William the intervening consultation sufficed to arm him with some fresh tactic.

"I would ask my worthy opponent if his vocabulary is exhausted by one word?" William asked, having returned to his podium before his question and gripping it with obvious displeasure.

The other candidate smiled at the question, though he immediately reached for his scratch pad. The arena became so quiet then that the scratching pencil on paper was perceptible to the ears of most everyone in the arena. The candidate finished and handed the paper to the moderator, who stood in waiting.

"This is most unusual I should say," said the recipient, "but there is nothing in our rules of agreement that would suggest I cannot read what he has written."

The moderator cleared his throat and read the words silently to himself first.

"The candidate writes: 'I can only speak one word, but I am at no loss because of it, because that one word is a needed word. If there is need for more explanation, I would direct questions to my doctor, who is in the audience.'"

A woman stood up immediately, as the candidate motioned for her to speak on his behalf.

"I object," said Norman, beside himself again over this latest bit of theatre. "The candidate is not allowed to have a second party speak for him; he must speak without aid of another!" he shouted.

Norman stood to approach the moderator, but the surrogate spoke over the objections of both.

"The candidate can only speak one word. A couple decades ago he ceased to say anything but the word and now can utter nothing but that needed word in our violent world. His tongue and mouth are now completely incapable of forming any other words. He could not advocate or fight even if he desired to. But his loss is our gain—if, that is, we accept his invitation."

Norman was exasperated and William no less so, but none of it mattered. The audience immediately stood when she finished and began to chant the monosyllable of their preferred candidate.

For the previous days Norman and William had despaired with minds ending up bleaker than the bare walls of their rented office. A vase of fresh cut flowers had sat on one desk, sent over by Norman's wife, at home alone, and with the depressing note that he and William were wasting their time. The flowers were meant to console them, she said with a telephone call afterward. Norman confessed to William that he hoped the election was not all he stood to lose; William's face fell as his expression portended worse.

"I don't know," William said. He shook his head and resumed perfunctory attention to the list of desperate measures they had concocted to upset the popular opponent. Their adversary had ridden waves of public adulation, while Norman and William dithered like field mice beneath the foundations of a shaking monument.

"I know!" Norman said, "Challenge him to a debate; he'll look like a fool!" Norman and William had a laugh then and one sorely needed. Norman continued to argue the idea, to work at persuading William to try it for want of anything better, until William, more out of exhaustion than enthusiasm, embraced the new plan and then threw away the scraps of paper previously scribbled on.

"Debate it is," William said, with no enthusiasm. "We might as well call him out anyway, so he can shoot us and be done with it, before they kill us," William added, more astute than Norman of the immensity of their climb against this opponent. Their opponent probably had no idea what a gun looked like, and certainly never contemplated any violence toward anyone, them included.

The opponent had immediately stood up when William and Norman entered the stage of the arena.

The man manifested no nervousness, and as Norman gazed at him and then at William, he started to feel revulsion for the idea he had proposed.

William would be slaughtered by this candidate, who acted more the part of a friend than any opponent should.

Norman began a private though gargantuan appeal to heaven with the earnestness of a man at the throes of execution, but his appeal stopped when the moderator asked both candidates to come together for a briefing on the rules of the debate.

There were three reporters from local media, both television and print, and they would ask half of the questions, and the audience, composed of some ordinary and some belligerent citizens, would have equal opportunity for questions.

The arena was packed as Norman had expected, but the time before the event too brief for him to flee the inevitable disaster, or for an overdose of nerve pills to take their lethal effect.

Perhaps he should have been the candidate, and not William, for William looked more nervous than a cornered rabbit surrounded by salivating hounds.

Norman appealed to heaven again.

William's opponent received huge applause at his introduction and Norman felt a deepening sense of doom after almost no audience members applauded his candidate.

The questions from media and audience rotated, and after a coin toss in his favor William received the choice whether he or his opponent would field the first question, and William looked at Norman like a drowning man looks for a straw. Norman signaled for him to take the question.

The question as expected was about the war, for it was everywhere around them and getting closer by the week. On occasion the distant rumblings could be heard when the wind was right, and the local population had tired of the effort of war and killing and particularly after witnessing some of their soldiers never returning.

Norman was mildly impressed when William's answer started the right way, and even after some unevenness in the middle of his answer, William managed to resume his strong beginning and went on to produce a stellar reply. Some in the audience looked on astounded and flummoxed, as if they had never before heard a cogent argument offered for war over worse alternatives. Norman looked on in disbelief, almost ashamed that he had doubted the tenacity of William to negotiate the debate with the opponent. Norman even glimpsed a small smile of satisfaction on the usually unexpressive face of William of the past months. It would be their last moment of elation.

The two candidates got two minutes to respond to questions, and William's answer having contained itself within the allotted one hundred twenty seconds, the opponent now had his turn with the same question and an identical amount of time.

"Peace peacc peace—"

The moderator looked fluxamed after the third repetition of the word, but it took him until the fifty-seventh repetition to decide what to do before he managed to interrupt the speaker, and by that time the candidate had produced thirty eight more repetitions of the word. The audience came to its feet then and for three minutes chorused the word before any order was restored.

"Gentlemen we came here to debate!" the moderator had shouted, but no one heard him, so he took up his gavel and after twenty-one strikes on his desk the noise had quieted enough for him to be heard, and so he repeated his words.

"Will this time of interruption be returned for my candidate to resume his answer?" The campaign manager for the peace candidate had asked the question, anxious that her candidate get at least thirty more repetitions before his allotted time expired, she said.

"Is he going to simply keep repeating that word?" the moderator asked.

"The candidate feels this is all he need say. He is prepared to repeat it, until we have it. As a man thinketh, so he speaketh; thus he doeth."

The roar of the approving audience behind her was deafening.

"Is he prepared to defend and debate that idea here tonight?" the moderator shouted over the audience, if such were possible.

"The candidate is prepared to continue doing what he is doing."

"And that is to repeat this word and nothing more?"

"Nothing more is necessary. I am requesting that you return the remainder of his response time back to him Mr. Moderator."

The moderator threw up his hand, and the candidate resumed.

"Peace peace

peace peace peace peace peace peace peace peace peace peace peace—"

After his time expired the monosyllabic candidate ceased to speak, and the moderator, though rattled by the shaky start to the debate, asked for another question, this time from the audience.

"I would like to ask both candidates a question that cuts to the heart of our dilemma: Do they regard peace as preferable to war?" The questioner sat back down in the audience and waited for the result.

In accordance with the rules of the debate, and William having gone first on the prior question, the peace candidate was allowed to respond first this time.

"Peace peace—" The candidate's words were stretched out this time and spoken with almost a second of pause between the final sound of the word and the beginning of the next.

"No doubt on how he is answering the question!" the moderator said, now apparently reconciled that the remainder of the evening was forging a will of its own. A huge cheer went up from the audience. William was noticeably shaken by what was happening, and he looked feebly toward Norman for any sign of a suggestion, or some hint of guidance on how to proceed, but Norman offered nothing except a face that told William he must stand on his own, and that the poor soul would have to make do alone.

When his turn finally came, William opened his mouth, but nothing would come out, and after a while the audience started to chant for his opponent.

"Peace peace—"

Two minutes before the end of any debate or town, the peace candidate tried to discourage the good natured fun of the crowd, who sent threatening gestures toward the only two faces in the arena not uttering the monosyllabic word of the community.

"Even the appearance of violence is to be avoided," the peace candidate wrote, though to no avail, as the gestures continued until the faces that hosted them melted away in the blast.